THE
GLORIOUS
PURSUIT

EMBRACING THE
VIRTUES *of* CHRIST

GARY L. THOMAS

NAVPRESS®
BRINGING TRUTH TO LIFE

OUR GUARANTEE TO YOU

The Navigators is an international Christian organization. Our mission is to advance the gospel of Jesus and His kingdom into the nations through spiritual generations of laborers living and discipling among the lost. We see a vital movement of the gospel, fueled by prevailing prayer, flowing freely through relational networks and out into the nations where workers for the kingdom are next door to everywhere.

NavPress is the publishing ministry of The Navigators. The mission of NavPress is to reach, disciple, and equip people to know Christ and make Him known by publishing life-related materials that are biblically rooted and culturally relevant. Our vision is to stimulate spiritual transformation through every product we publish.

© 1998 by Gary Thomas
All rights reserved. No part of this publication may be reproduced in any form without written permission from NavPress, P.O. Box 35001, Colorado Springs, CO 80935.

ISBN-10: 1-57683-052-7
ISBN-13: 978-1-57683-052-9

Cover Illustration by Nicholas Wilton\ Stock Illustration Source

Some of the anecdotal illustrations in this book are true to life and are included with the permission of the persons involved. All other illustrations are composites of real situations, and any resemblance to people living or dead is coincidental.

Unless otherwise identified, all Scripture quotations in this publication are taken from the HOLY BIBLE: NEW INTERNATIONAL VERSION® (NIV®). Copyright ©1973, 1978, 1984 by International Bible Society. Used by permission of Zondervan Publishing House. All rights reserved. Other versions used include: The Message: New Testament with Psalms and Proverbs (MSG) by Eugene H. Peterson, copyright © 1993, 1994, 1995, used by permission of NavPress Publishing Group; and the New King James Version (NKJV), copyright © 1979, 1980, 1982, 1990, Thomas Nelson Inc., Publishers.

Thomas, Gary (Gary Lee)
        The glorious pursuit: embracing the virtues of Christ / Gary
Thomas.
            p. cm.
        Includes bibliographical references.   98-8737
        ISBN 1-57683-052-7 (pbk.)   CIP
        1. Virtues.   2. Christian life.   I. Title.
BV4630.T48 1998
241'.4—dc21

Printed in the United States of America

5 6 7 8 9 10 11 12 13 / 11 10 09 08 07

Published in association with the literary agency of Alive Communications, Inc., 7680 Goddard Street, Suite 200, Colorado Springs, CO 80920 (www.alivecommunications.com).

FOR A FREE CATALOG OF NAVPRESS BOOKS & BIBLE STUDIES, CALL
1-800-366-7788 (USA) OR 1-800-839-4769 (CANADA).

To my parents, E.J. and Geneva Thomas,
and my in-laws, Bill and Marilyn Ehli,
with tremendous gratitude and great respect

CONTENTS

ACKNOWLEDGMENTS

Without my editor, David Hazard, this book would never have been started, much less completed. He approached me about the subject and coached me through the process. I am deeply indebted to him. In addition to David, I'm very thankful for the hard work put in by Lori Mitchell, Sue Geiman, and Nanci McAlister at NavPress.

To Dr. Bob Stone, I owe a great spiritual debt for his inspiration, prayers, and friendship. The body of Hillcrest Chapel surrounded our family as we returned to Washington state, making the completion of this book possible.

Several people played key roles at various moments in the composition of this book, offering suggestions and helpful critiques: Terry Glaspey, Dan Little, Dr. Don Whitney, and Evan Howard. Others provided help and encouragement in many other ways. Rob and Jill Takemura, Roger and Deb Ellefson, Doug and Susan Thorson, Gene Breitenbach, and Brady Bobbink.

A special thanks to Kathy Yanni, my agent for this book.

Additionally, I owe a great deal to a family that makes this life possible (and enjoyable). I have leaned heavily on my wife, Lisa, throughout this process and, as always, I am tremendously grateful for the blessing of being a father to Allison, Graham, and Kelsey. Their understanding of my calling has made working out of our home a tremendous blessing.

Finally, and most importantly, it was a particularly rewarding experience for me to walk with God through the writing of this book. So many little "providences" contributed to what found its way in that I never lost the feeling of writing this book in partnership with Him. If any of the insights contained herein prove helpful, thanks should be offered to the true vine and gardener (John 15:1-8). Apart from Him, we can do nothing.

GENERAL INTRODUCTION

by Dallas Willard

The SPIRITUAL FORMATION LINE presents discipleship to Jesus Christ as the greatest opportunity individual human beings have in life and the only hope corporate mankind has of solving its insurmountable problems.

It affirms the unity of the present-day Christian with those who walked beside Jesus during His incarnation. To be His disciple then was to be with Him, to learn to be like Him. It was to be His student or apprentice in kingdom living. His disciples heard what He said and observed what He did; then, under His direction, they simply began to say and do the same things. They did so imperfectly but progressively. As He taught: "Everyone who is fully trained will be like his teacher" (Luke 6:40).

Today it is the same, except now it is the resurrected Lord who walks throughout the world. He invites us to place our confidence in Him. Those who rely on Him believe that He knows how to live and will pour His life into us as we "take His yoke . . . and learn from Him, for He is gentle and humble in heart" (Matthew 11:29, emphasis added). To take His yoke means joining Him in His work, making our work His work. To trust Him is to understand that total immersion in what He is doing with our life is the best thing that could ever happen to us.

To "learn from Him" in this total-life immersion is how we "seek first his kingdom and his righteousness" (Matthew 6:33). The outcome is that we increasingly are able to do all things, speaking or acting, as if Christ were doing them (Colossians 3:17). As apprentices of Christ we are not learning how to do some special religious activity, but how to live every moment of our lives from the reality of God's kingdom. I am learning how to live my actual life as Jesus would if He were me.

If I am a plumber, clerk, bank manager, homemaker, elected official, senior citizen, or migrant worker, I am in "full-time" Christian service no less than someone who earns his or her living in a specifically religious role. Jesus stands beside me and teaches me in all I do to live in God's world. He shows me how, in every circumstance, to reside in His Word and thus be a genuine apprentice of His—His disciple indeed. This enables me to find the reality of God's world everywhere I may be, and thereby to escape from enslavement to sin and evil (John 8:31-32). We become able to do what we know to be good and right, even when it is humanly impossible. Our lives and words become constant testimony of the reality of God.

A plumber facing a difficult plumbing job must know how to integrate it into the kingdom of God as much as someone attempting to win another to Christ or preparing a lesson for a congregation. Until we are clear on this, we will have missed Jesus' connection between life and God and will automatically exclude most of our everyday lives from the domain of faith and discipleship. Jesus lived most of His life on earth as a blue-collar worker, someone we might describe today as an "independent contractor." In His vocation He practiced everything He later taught about life in the kingdom.

The "words" of Jesus I primarily reside in are those recorded in the New Testament Gospels. In His presence, I learn the goodness of His instructions and how to carry them out. It is not a matter of meriting life from above, but of receiving that life concretely in my circumstances. Grace, we must learn, is opposed to earning, not to effort.

For example, I move away from using derogatory language against others, calling them twits, jerks, or idiots (Matthew 5:22), and increasingly mesh with the respect and endearment for persons that naturally flows from God's way. This in turn transforms all of my dealings with others into tenderness and makes the usual coldness and brutality of human relations, which lays a natural foundation for abuse and murder, simply unthinkable.

Of course, the "learning of Him" is meant to occur in the context of His people. They are the ones He commissioned to make disciples, surround them in the reality of the triune name, and teach them to do "everything I have commanded you" (Matthew 28:20). But the disciples we make are His disciples, never ours. We are His apprentices along with them. If we are a little farther along the way, we can only echo the apostle Paul: "Follow my example, as I follow the example of Christ" (1 Corinthians 11:1).

It is a primary task of Christian ministry today, and of those who write for this line of books, to reestablish Christ as a living teacher in the midst of His people. He has been removed by various historical developments: assigned the role of mere sacrifice for sin or social prophet and martyr. But where there is no teacher, there can be no students or disciples.

If we cannot be His students, we have no way to learn to exist always and everywhere within the riches and power of His Word. We can only flounder along as if we were on our own so far as the actual details of our lives are concerned. That is where multitudes of well-meaning believers find themselves today. But that is not the intent of Him who says, "Come to me . . . and you will find rest for your souls" (Matthew 11:28-29).

Each book in this line is designed to contribute to this renewed vision of Christian spiritual formation and to illuminate what apprenticeship to Jesus Christ means within all the specific dimensions of human existence. The mission of these books is to form the whole person so that the nature of Christ becomes the natural expression of our souls, bodies, and spirits throughout our daily lives.

INTRODUCTION

Many Christians carry a deep grief, or at least a dissatisfaction, about themselves and their experience of God. Can I be a better person? How can God be a more real presence in my life?

The scriptures make it plain that God wants to restore us to a place in the order of creation from which we fell—that is, to our place as sons and daughters of God (John 1:12,13). Beyond His work to save us, the father also wants to restore our innermost being—the core of beliefs, attitudes, and motives that is the face of our inner man —His own likeness.

It is this singular concept that lies at the heart of NavPress's publishing efforts in this Spiritual Formation Line. This is a gradual, not an instantaneous transformation, in which God has a part . . . and we have one too.

Jesus said, "My father is always at His work" (John 5:17). And so it is His effort that first awakens us to His reality and presence, that shows us the destructiveness of sin and the futility of life without Him. This effort—God's movement toward us—we call *grace*. By grace we are saved. And it is grace that gives us the power to grow and change, until, as Paul says, we become "mirrors, brightly reflecting the glory of God."

But what does the invisible God look like? How would we know when we are beginning, even in the smallest way, to resemble Him?

For centuries, Christians have understood that the very image of God could be seen in the spirit of His only begotten Son, Jesus Christ (Hebrews 1:3). Look into the person of Jesus and you will begin to see Him who is invisible in radiant qualities of character, like *humility, patience, selfless love.* . . . The early and late Church fathers, from Cyprian to Augustine, pick up on Paul's admonition that we be "imitators of God" (Ephesians 5:1), with the goal of growing in these interior qualities. The theme is carried in such classics of the middle ages as à Kempis's *The Imitation of Christ* and Bernard of Clairvaux's treatises, and more recently in almost all of Andrew Murray's books, especially his small treasure, *Humility*. The qualities they knew and wrote about were also known as the spiritual "virtues" of Christ.

That brings us to our part: It's clear that, throughout Church history, Christians have understood that as God works around us, and in us, our part is to *respond* to Him so that we might be changed. How? By consciously, daily, giving Him fuller access to our core of attitude and will, that became misshapen around a core of self-centeredness. By joining our own efforts to God's, as He reshapes our inner man to the character qualities we see in Christ Himself. And so it is that the virtues of Christ—His humility, fortitude, love, self-control and the like—begin to appear in the midst of our everyday rubs, conflicts, challenges, and demands . . . and we start to "shine among men" (Matthew 5:15).

Gary Thomas explores for us many of the central "virtues" that shine so brilliantly in Christ Jesus. He walks us through common situations God uses to nudge us, and calls us to respond by letting the goodness of His divine nature shine through. For this reason, we are pleased to include this volume in our Spiritual Formation Line, trusting it will help you in the most "glorious pursuit" of life . . . the chance to experience the life of transformation, as the character of Christ grows in you.

DAVID HAZARD
Editor
SPIRITUAL FORMATION LINE

THE SOUL OF
SPIRITUAL FORMATION

CHAPTER ONE

GETTING YOUR LIFE BACK

Once you let God into you,
you have God in you.
And God is a dynamo.
PETER KREEFT

O N AUGUST 20, 1949, A RATHER BIZARRE HEADLINE APPEARED ON the front page of the Washington Post: "Priest Frees Mount Ranier Boy Reported Held in Devil's Grip." Though the exorcism took place in St. Louis, the story made top billing in the Post because the thirteen-year-old boy was a native of Mount Ranier, Maryland, a small town in the shadow of Washington, D.C.

The boy, "Robbie," had developed a close relationship with a spiritualist aunt. After the aunt died, objects started flying around the room in Robbie's presence. Robbie's family turned to their priest, Father Luther Miles Schulze of St. Stephen's Evangelical Lutheran Church in Washington, D.C., for help. Somewhat skeptical, Schulze took Robbie into his own home for observation. In Schulze's presence, the bed that Robbie was lying on began to shake. Schulze put the mattress on the floor. With Robbie still lying on top of it, the mattress glided back up onto the bed.

Rattled, Schulze referred the family to the St. James Catholic Church, also in Washington, saying that Robbie's situation was something "the Roman Catholics understand."

A young Roman Catholic priest undertook the rite of exorcism and paid dearly for his inexperience. During the rite, Robbie ripped a spring from the bed and slashed the priest from shoulder to wrist, a wound requiring over one hundred stitches to close. The young cleric gave up in frustration.

Robbie's family eventually took him to St. Louis, where he was placed under the care of Father William B. Bowdern, who was granted permission to initiate the rite of exorcism. Six weeks of grueling spiritual battle ensued, but on Easter Monday, April 18, 1949, Robbie was freed.

Too many reputable priests and medical professionals testified to Robbie's situation for us to dismiss it as one man's hallucination or as religious sensationalism. Father Bowdern would later be consulted on over two hundred cases of alleged demonic possession. He didn't find a single one to be valid—ample evidence that he was not frivolous in citing demonic influence.

Though Robbie lost all memory of the events, the same is not true of his former Maryland neighbors. The house that Robbie's family had lived in soon became known as the "Devil's House," and after Robbie and his family moved on to St. Louis, the city had an unsalable eyesore on its hands. No one went near the place.

Eventually, Mount Ranier officials decided to turn the place into a park and build a children's gazebo. Aware of the fear and superstition that follows such events, the city completely demolished the house and even dug deeply around it, then leveled the hole with trucked-in, new dirt.

On the spot where a young man lived in spiritual darkness, children now run and play tag as families take walks and eat picnics. A place once forsaken, unusable, was given new life.

In a sense, this gives a vivid picture of what God wants to do for us. We need not be possessed by demons to need deliverance from the imprisonment of a self-centered life. Many have hoped for this change to come in a moment in time we call "conversion." Yet most of us have found that we need more than initial conversion because the hoped-for freedoms and changes did not come. Or they showed themselves briefly and then slid away from us.

The truth is, we need a process of renewal, a deep digging and infilling of our souls with something new so that on the site of our former life, a new life stands. We want God to take us—people who are stuck in old habits, trapped in the living death of boredom or irrelevance, possessed by our own possessions—and to deliver us from ourselves by a long miracle of spiritual transformation. We need Him to dig out those abrasive aspects of our character and replace them with a refreshing vitality, ultimately creating a new personality — the promised life of Christ in us.

God designed us to be His image bearers, each of us reflecting a particular aspect of Himself. He is eager to "deliver" each of us from ourselves and create a "new man" in us, as C. S. Lewis points out in his modern classic, *The Screwtape Letters.* As Screwtape, the mentor demon, explains to Wormwood, his protégé, "When [God] talks of their losing their selves, He only means abandoning the clamor of self-will; once they have done that, He really gives them back all their personality, and boasts (I am afraid, sincerely) that when they are wholly His they will be more themselves than ever."[1]

Pause a moment and try to imagine yourself as a person who acts with the compassion of Christ; who has the patience of God Himself; who is discerning; gentle, yet confident; surrendered to the will and purpose of God. This is the life Jesus wants you to inherit, transforming you into a person who is motivated by the beautiful, not the lustful; the generous, not the selfish; the noble, not the conniving; the creative, not the destructive.

Is this the person you want to become? If so, there is an ancient and biblical practice by which the image and nature of God are restored in you. For centuries, Christian teachers spoke about "the practice of the virtues of Christ," meaning the process of growth in the spiritual character qualities of Christ. Thomas à Kempis's thirteenth-century work, *The Imitation of Christ,* became a classic "handbook" for spiritual growth, as did John Climacus's *Ladder of Divine Ascent,* Teresa of Avila's *Interior Castle,* and *The Ascent of Mount Carmel* by John of the Cross. It was not assumed that the "new life" from above would come to instantaneous fruition, but that it would result gradually from the reshaping of the inner man.

Conversion is just the *beginning* of the Christian life. Spiritual formation — rooted in the virtues — must follow. As we put our faith in Christ and walk with Him, He changes us from within. That's what spiritual formation means — being *formed,* spiritually. While salvation is a work that is done entirely within God's mercy and without human effort (Romans 9:16), growth in Christ involves a cooperation between God and His children (1 John 3:3; Philippians 2:12-13). And just as body builders use weights to shape their physiques, so Christians of the past "worked out" by practicing the virtues. They didn't expect holiness to "suddenly appear" just because they had prayed a prayer of salvation. Instead, they understood spiritual formation as an intentional process. This is what James was talking about when he wrote, "Perseverance must finish its work so that you may be mature and complete, not lacking anything" (James 1:4).

Plato argued that there were four virtues—wisdom, courage, temperance, and justice—to which Medieval teachers added the three "theological" virtues—faith, hope, and love. Past Christian teachers often preferred to speak of the "virtues" of Jesus rather than aspire to abstract ideals of goodness. Virtues to them meant a certain set of spiritual attributes, or heart attitudes, that describe the inner life of the Lord.

That's what we mean by virtue in this discussion—inner orientations and behaviors evidenced in the life of Jesus while He walked on earth. A virtue is displayed when we choose to serve rather than dominate or manipulate; when we choose to respect rather than lust or harm; when we choose to be gentle rather that abrupt. Choosing virtue is choosing to submit our will to God and to act like Jesus would act.

Practicing a vice means being ruled by the power of self. A vice-ruled life is prone to chaotic outbursts of anger, selfishness, and destruction—the opposite of the orderly and disciplined life that God calls us to. Vice enthrones the self—"I'll act however I *want* to act, making myself in my own image." This life, as we'll see, is a self-defeating life. While the virtues bring spiritual health, the vices are a spiritual cancer, destroying us from within.

The list of virtues chosen for this book has been based on the virtues recognized throughout the ages, though I make no claim that it is anywhere near exhaustive. Some well-known virtues (hope, for one) are not addressed. But the ones discussed here will certainty suffice to help you begin your exploration into the life-changing and spirit-transforming world of the virtues.

The virtues we will discuss were readily seen in the life of Jesus. Chief among the virtues was *humility*, for Jesus left His position beside the Father and humbled Himself, taking the lowest position of all as the suffering servant for the whole human race. The practice of humility was, and is, the lifelong, arduous work of remembering our place beneath the authority and sovereignty of God who, though He has welcomed us as beloved children, is still God.

Other virtues of Jesus include *surrender* to the will and purposes of God; *detachment* from our dependence on worldly securities; *love* that's clear of self-interest; *chastity* that springs from purity of heart; *generosity*; and keeping *vigilance* over our souls (for out of the heart come the forces that determine our life). Also *patience,* or enduring with ourselves and others in the long haul of growth and challenge; *discernment,* by which we learn to perceive God with the eyes of the soul; *thankfulness* in all things, for we see all things coming to us from the hand of God; *gentleness*; and *fortitude* to continue in spirit when people and circumstances turn against us. And along with these, *obedience* as we cooperate with God's unfolding will; and *penitence,* by which we actively correct the errors we've made and redress the harms we've caused. (Though it is true Jesus was without sin, we are not. Therefore, penitence was included in the list of classic Christian virtues for the sake of fallen men and women, which includes each one of us.)

The virtues were understood to be the heart attitudes by which Jesus, as a man, showed us how to stay in right relationship to God and to others. As Christians grew in these spiritual attributes of Jesus, real change took place in their character. And so spiritual growth was measured in the maturing of a person's character, not only in, say, his or her knowledge of Scripture or doctrine. And change, to be real and lasting, was known to proceed from a transformed heart.

POLLUTED VIRTUES

Unfortunately, "practicing the virtues of Christ" has a polluted history. In some centuries, virtues were used as measuring sticks to make Christians feel guilty and inferior. In other times, practices like humility and penitence were imposed on people as obligations. And so we look back and see garish things in church history—people flogging themselves in public as acts of so-called humiliation and repentance. What a tragic misunderstanding of practices that were meant to begin in the innermost chambers of our being, not as superficial demonstrations, to empower us from the soul to find freedom from our old self-centeredness and sin.

In better times, Christians understood that they could learn to practice the virtues as part of a literal school in godliness.

There was no mystery to this, no esoteric knowledge to uncover.

It did require a fundamental understanding of the basic patterns of spiritual growth. Our forebears understood that, at the time of conversion, there is a gap between our ideals and the reality of our behavior. Today, we may want to hide from, or deny, this fact. We may believe that a Christian should change instantly at conversion (or shortly thereafter). We want to skirt the long, arduous process of real spiritual growth and development. The ancients weren't fooled; they saw the hard but rewarding work of character transformation as the normal pathway of every Christian's experience. Common sense tells us that bad habits take time to lose and good habits take time to develop. If someone is willing to learn and to be transformed from the inside out, they will eventually see true, long-lasting changes.

If you mention "virtues" today, however, many people — even some Christians — assume you are talking about a sex-less, pleasure-less, colorless existence. Just as our understanding of Puritanism has been distorted into a ridiculous caricature of what it really was, so virtuous living has been defined by what it is *not:* "Virtue means you can't do this, that, or the other." The ancient reality, however, presents biblical virtue as a positive life — what you can *become.*

The life Christ wants to grow in you is not founded on a list of do's and dont's, and it cannot be accurately measured by our current yardsticks of spiritual performance standards — by how much you do or do not witness, or read your Bible, or attend church. And it is most definitely not a life of striving as you compare yourself to someone else. It is the slow dawning of the life and characteristics of Jesus Christ, who lives in you and who wants to grow more evident in you.

Learning how to grow in the spiritual characteristics of Christ does not take your life from you. In ancient times, it was understood as God's preferred method of giving you your life back. The virtues are, quite literally, God's sculpting tools by which He shapes us into the image of His Son. To experience His life in us is to find our way into the life Jesus promised when He said, "I have come that [you] may have life, and have it to the full."[2]

No, we'll never experience *all* of eternal life on this planet. Sinless perfection and complete transformation are not possible here. But it *is* possible for us to radically reflect the very nature of Jesus Christ, and in this sense, live life "to the full."

A LIFE MISSPENT, OR WELL SPENT?

"Jennifer" looked horrified when I told her about a college reunion I was planning to attend.

"What?" I asked.

"There's no way I could face all those people again, considering the way I behaved. I wish I could wipe those four years off the pages of history."

Because Jennifer lived without regard to virtue, she created a season of regret rather than memories to treasure. This is what we're talking about when we suggest that God wants to give us our life back.

How sad it would be to say at the end of your life, as does a character in one of C. S. Lewis's novels, "I now see that I spent most of my life in doing neither what I ought nor what I liked."[3] Instead of spending your days with regret, growing in the virtues of Christ will help you to live a meaningful, focused, and selfless life.

Virtue allows us to live with an intact reputation, an energizing sense of zeal, and an abiding enjoyment of life. Peter Kreeft refers to the life of godly virtue as "health of soul."[4] Isn't that a marvelous thought? God wants you to have a healthy soul! Learning how to practice the virtues of Christ won't get you from earth into heaven, but it will bring the life-giving power of heaven to earth.

In the next two chapters, we'll explore the dynamics and nature of how we are transformed from the inside out through the virtues and presence of Christ. Later, we'll explore the individual virtues one by one, examining their importance and demonstrating simple ways to practice them in daily life.

In this, we seek to recover a lost art—the time-tested, life-proven, rock-solid knowledge, practiced by the ancients, that the school of virtues really works.

Have you been looking for change? Life from within? Spiritual strength to face life's demands and challenges? The knowledge of God's presence with you . . . and in you?

Transformation and growth in Christ are possible. They are the promise of God and your heritage. They are the new life for the soul you have been hoping for, the proven method through which God will give you your life back.

CHAPTER TWO

THE HOLY BRIDGE

*This life therefore, is not righteousness, but growth in
righteousness, not health but healing, not being but
becoming, not rest but exercise. We are not yet what we
shall be, but we are growing toward it; the process is not yet
finished but it is going on. This is not the end but it is the
road; all does not yet gleam in glory but all is being purified.*

MARTIN LUTHER[1]

—◀○▶—

I T HAD BEEN AN EXHAUSTING WEEK FOR ME, WITH TWO OR THREE
more hard weeks ahead. I was flying from coast to coast, so I
requested an aisle seat. I needed the room to get some work done.

"Sorry, sir," the agent said, "all that remain are center seats."

"Are you kidding me? The plane's full?"

"Afraid so."

I sighed as I got in line to board, knowing work would be impossible. I dug a book out of my shoulder bag and found my seat between
a fairly big man and an elderly woman.

I didn't even have my seat belt on when the woman started talking. "Do you live in California?"

"No, I was here on business."

She was probably in her seventies, with a sweet demeanor. The
universal grandmother. But I was tired from speaking at several events,
and I looked wistfully at the book in my hands. Escape was buried in
those pages, but how could I open the cover without being rude?

"I'm sorry," the woman said, perhaps catching my glance. "I'm
sure you probably want to read."

I smiled politely and began to crack open my book.

"I just don't get to talk very much," she said quietly. "Not since my husband died fifteen years ago."

Her words were like a spiritual body-slam. I was tired, full of self-pity about some personal pressures I was under, and selfishly demanding four hours of duty-free living on a cross-country flight. Still . . . a thought occurred to me. Out of all the seats I could have been assigned, events had been so ordered that I was seated next to this elderly woman who was alone and hoping for someone to talk to. Wasn't it at least *possible* that God had placed me beside her for four hours?

"I'm sorry to hear about your husband," I said, putting my book away. "Do you have any children?"

Her face lit up a little, and the conversation took off. I did my best to draw her out, to ask her opinions, to get a glimpse of her life. I found out she was a Christian and that her church had been facing some difficult times.

I listened a lot, even though the novel kept summoning me. "This is God's daughter," I kept reminding myself. "She deserves to have someone care about what she's going through."

And as the flight ended, a surprising thing happened. As I stepped off the plane I felt — no other word to describe it — *buoyant*. A simple act of surrendering to the situation in which God had placed me ushered me into an inner reality in which I could practically taste the presence of Christ, amazingly renewed inside. The pressures were the same but not so heavy on my spirit.

What had taken place? Considering it now, I see this: I'd surrendered to the situation, believing it was not a random circumstance denying me the time to do what I wanted to do, but a situation in which God had placed me. I had decided to act on a higher claim than my own personal agenda or comfort. I recognized my position under the guidance and direction of the Father, which is the essence of the virtue of *humility*. And I *surrendered* my will to His will. In doing so, I experienced Jesus. Since Jesus is the true delight of my soul, it was only natural that I should feel a quiet elation.

That is one of many common experiences in which I have understood how the practice of the virtues is a highway to experiencing Jesus. To some that may seem a dangerous statement, and yet it's true. Just as mystics pursue God through contemplative prayer, so we can enter God's presence through the practice of the virtues of Christ.[2]

When we talk about "experiencing" God, we're faced with two tensions. There will always be Christians who insist they experience Him in the "inner" world of their soul, through prayer, contemplation, solitude, and quiet, or through the thrills of religious fervor. And on the other side are the Christians who insist the "experience" of God comes through our acts of obedience and service in the "outer" world or in a more cerebral sense, as they encounter the Word of God.

But there are problems and limitations in these viewpoints. Stress outer behavior too much, and you often create perfectionistic legalists—people out of touch with the empowering grace of God and His mercy. Stress Bible knowledge to the exclusion of other things, and you get Christians with a roster of right doctrines in their head but with little heart concern for living out what they know. And again, stress interior experiences too much, and you can end in a personal search for "enlightenment" that does not build the self-giving character of Christ. Cut loose from the authority of Scripture, personal experience becomes God. You can become the kind of hypocrite who takes secret pride in their illuminated and "higher" experiences, and as a result they cannot find their place in the common, serving, body of Christ.

Imitating the virtues of Christ can *connect* the inner reality of our soul with the everyday practicality of our *outer* behavior. I said, "Okay, God, I'll accept your call on my life at this moment." An inner attitude led me to a particular action—putting down my book and directing my attention to another child of God who needed some care and spirit lifting. And the result was that I experienced the pleasure of cooperating with God, under His direction, in a work He had for me to do.

Almost selfishly now, I am more alert to these divine appointments. Just recently, I asked an elderly woman if I could carry her heavy bag. She was surprised . . . and delighted. "I've spent my entire life caring for others," she said, "and I can't believe that someone is carrying *my* bag."

Without the interior sense that Christ is living His life in me, however, lugging heavy bags for strangers would be a joyless, religious duty. (You wind up asking yourself, "Have I lugged *enough* suitcases? Have I lugged any *lately?"*) But in fact, the experience itself is transformed. It's not that I want more tally marks of service; I want to know more of Christ, not in head knowledge but in heart knowledge. I have come to want what James talks about: "Religion that God our Father accepts as pure and faultless is this: to look after orphans and widows in their distress and to keep oneself from being polluted by the world" (James 1:27). I've begun to see that God makes the blessing of His presence known to those who take this verse literally, and I want that blessing.

I have returned from business trips with great regrets, and I have returned from business trips experiencing the joy of life in Christ, and I know which one I want. The virtues have become my bridge to help me return with a sense of fulfillment instead of regret. Regret is a debilitating spiritual drain — MS of the soul.

Have you been plagued by regret? I'm not just talking about sin here. The absence of Christ's life in us can feel like a living death, which creates a passive regret. Many of us accept the restraints and limitations of a life ruled by otherwise good biblical principles and morals. But without healthy interior growth, we are still stuck with all the diseases of a normal, fallen soul. Self-absorption, apathy, boredom, sin, and failure — any number of spiritual illnesses can keep us from feeling fully alive spiritually.

Are you feeling depleted, like you're bored with Christianity? Or tired of trying to measure up as a Christian? Wishing you had a sense of Christ's reality in your life? If that's your situation, learning how to grow in the virtues of Christ can be a bridge to the new life you have wanted.

CHRIST IN YOU

Some time ago, I caught myself stewing in some destructive attitudes. For instance, I displayed constant irritation at people over petty things: Bad customer service in stores. Being cut off by thoughtless drivers in traffic. One time I was singing a worship chorus to myself in a store, and it made me feel like a hypocrite. Either I was going to have to lose the attitude or lose the chorus. I opted to lose the attitude.

The route I took to change was a gradual one. I thought, "What if I adopted another mindset?" I didn't want to become a Christian

Pollyanna: "Gee, Lord, I'm so incredibly grateful that traffic was heavy and I missed my plane today. I really *love* this character growth stuff." That would have been play-acting, doomed to failure. But I did need to face up to the gap between my surliness and the spirit and character of Christ.

So I began by offering up to the Lord the inner stresses I felt. Each time I set out, I chose an attitude of acceptance. I accepted the fact that I might get caught by every red light, that the people serving me might have their own limitations and hassles. I dropped the unrealistic view that this is an easy world where everything *should* go right, meaning "right" according to my plan. Instead, I relaxed in the biblical view that this is a fallen world where unnerving things happen. When I began my day, I forced my mind off myself, my demands, and my own goals. I began to think a little about giving God a place in my demanding schedule: How could I make other people's experiences more pleasant, perhaps with a smile, an offer of assistance, or patience at the check-out line? Instead of scowling at slow-moving checkers—"Hey, buddy, why don't you buy a pulse and get some life in you?"—I started commending efficient checkers.

I made an important commitment to my own spiritual growth in Christ. This was a commitment to character growth and to making a place in my life for the virtues that describe Jesus to become, little by little, real in me.

One day, some time after I began this practice, I was hurrying down an aisle at a discount superstore. Kelsey, my youngest child, was talking to me, the store was crowded, and I was distracted with trying to find a book I needed. I also needed to get out of that place and could feel myself getting a little irritable.

I was scanning the shelves when I nearly collided with a woman coming the other way. I looked up at her . . . and instead of the old rush of irritation I felt something else. What I saw was not an obstacle or an irritation, a reduced version of a human being. I saw a person, who, like me, could use an encounter with kindness and grace in flesh form.

"I'm sorry to be in your way," the woman said, looking embarrassed.

"Not at all," I answered. "I'm just as much in your way as you're in mine. Here, let me move."

After the woman moved on, Kelsey, who had observed the encounter, said, "Daddy, why are you always so kind?"

Always so kind. . . . I laughed sheepishly. More are the times I've been very glad that Kelsey wasn't with me. But in this instance, I was thankful for the change in me that was noticeable, and perhaps the beginning of a new pattern that would be a witness to my daughter that Christ is real enough to change her irritable dad into a man of patience and peace.

My discoveries about growth began when I realized other people do not "make" me irritable — or anything else. They only bring out the inner man that has been secretly marinating in the juices of irritability. How about you? Are you blaming other people or other things for the responses to life that come out of you? Or do you need to stop and face honestly what is going on in your innermost being? What small piece of your life do you need to focus on?

When we take the time to get down to the real roots of our failure to grow in Christ, the truth emerges. And because we are fallen people — redeemed, but still needing to grow — spiritual growth turns out to be a lot of work. But wasn't salvation supposed to be free? After Jesus came into our hearts, wasn't He supposed to grow us up?

POTENT GRACE

Many Christians mistakenly think God will do all the work of spiritual growth for us. After all, aren't we "saved by grace, not by works?" That is true of the specific act of salvation. But grace is more than pardon. It is also the power God gives us to grow and change. Interacting with grace requires something of us because you and I also can turn away or resist grace.

Grace is often evident in the early days of our spiritual growth when it can seem as if we are being carried along. The first changes come swiftly and easily for many people and, compared to the dark, despairing attitudes we once had, our new sense of hope is bright and revolutionary. So we're tempted to conclude that spiritual growth must come from God's efforts.

In this technical age when so much work is done for us, it's easy to see how we get this wrong impression.

Not long ago, my seven-year-old son, Graham, approached me. "Will you play a game with me, Dad?" He had just rented a Super

Nintendo™ baseball game. I'm not a big fan of these games, but I *am* a big fan of Graham, so I consented.

He was the Mariners, and I was the White Sox. He explained the control buttons to me, and then he threw out the first pitch. After the first inning, I was ahead 5-0. After the second, 9-0. Graham was shocked. I was hitting the ball at will and throwing strikes past him with a brilliant array of pitches.

The last time Graham was this quiet, we were burying a dead terrapin. I looked at his silent face and suddenly my prideful euphoria was transformed into a father's empathy. *Maybe I should let up on him a little*, I thought.

I tried to bunt but watched my player hit the ball into left field. Acting on a hunch, I took my fingers off the buttons and watched my man get another hit.

"Uh, Graham," I said.

"Yeah?"

"You're not playing me. You're playing the computer. You must have pressed one player only."

Graham's enthusiasm for life returned instantaneously. "No wonder you were beating me!" he shouted, his excitement and relief translating into sheer volume. "I couldn't figure it out!"

For two innings, I had been amazed at my precise timing, my good eye, my dutiful fielding. But then I realized it hadn't been me at all. I was pushing buttons, but a kid's computer was doing all the work, ignoring my commands and going ahead on its own.

Spiritually, the same thing often happens to us. During certain stages of spiritual growth, it's as if we're on autopilot. Old habits drop away. Prayer and seeking God is new and exciting, no effort at all. Maybe after a special retreat or seminar you sensed God's nearness in a special way. Perhaps your eyes were opened to the needs of others, and you enjoyed the sense of doing His will in simple, everyday matters. In those times, you felt so in tune, so in control, on the fast track to maturity. And then . . .

One day, it seems as if the autopilot switch is turned off. I look back on earlier seasons in my life, and I wonder why I did not struggle *then* with some of the things I struggle with *now*. I was less mature then, wasn't I? I knew less then, didn't I, in terms of scriptural knowledge *and* common sense about life?

We cannot lose sight of the fact that our transformation into the spiritual likeness of Christ must go deep, to the core of our being. We are nothing like the Lord when we start out, though some of our surface "niceness" might trick us into thinking so. In fact, some change does come easily, quickly—especially surface attitudes, and especially when we are already very tired of repeating a behavior that's getting us nowhere. But the deeper, lasting character changes we need seem to come with time, involvement, effort, and even wrestling on our part.

This does not downplay God's active role of moving upon us to spotlight areas of our life which need to be brought under His truth and surrendered to the Spirit of Christ. But it does highlight our part in responding to grace.

After the moment of salvation, a Christian needs to be taught how to cooperate with God's work as He empowers us to grow and change. Our failure to teach this has resulted in a landscape littered with frustrated Christians who feel depleted or ineffective in the depths of their being. Are you one of them?

You might be a man who is reading this book after your latest fiery outburst against your wife or children. Though you are a Christian, your temper has gotten the best of you once again, and the pained looks on your children's faces make you realize that you are acting like a monster. Can God empower you with the peace and love of Christ, not only to make you a witness of Christ's presence to the world, but to keep you from wrecking your family?

Perhaps you're a woman who is just realizing that time logged in church doesn't equal maturity in the Christian faith. By now, you had hoped to be "a woman of God," someone whom younger women would seek out for spiritual guidance. Instead, you live with doubts and fears, and reflect, "I thought that becoming a Christian would help me to know God . . . to become a new creature in Christ. But I still have so many of the insecurities and doubts I had before."

It's also highly possible that you are in a state of spiritual exhaustion. Fighting hard to keep bad habits, negative attitudes, and temptations under control is not unlike trying to keep a hundred beach balls submerged. As soon as you push one down, another pops up. After a while, you feel no holier, just a lot more tired. You are thinking, *Where is the peace and rest, the freedom from guilt in God's presence, that I was promised in the gospel?*

After salvation, we all share a common need—a growing interior connection with God resulting in a lasting, outward change. Thankfully, the changes we see in our lives reinforce the power and beauty of interior growth. That's where growth takes place, where our inner and outer worlds cooperate and push each other forward.

The good news of the gospel is that we don't have to be slaves to the darkness and weakness within us. Growth and change, however, do not come easily. They require an effort on our part, but it must be the right kind of effort.

Perhaps this talk of "effort" already has made you feel let down and disappointed. You may be one of the many Christians today who are tired from striving to be good and fighting against certain sins, tired of trying to act nice all the time while living in a selfish, greedy world. If this is your experience, you may be thinking, "I can't possibly try any harder."

Learning to practice the attitudes or virtues of Christ does not begin with "trying hard to be better." It begins with a close, clear-eyed look at your true heart attitudes. Then comes a surrender of these attitudes to our merciful Father, who always welcomes us to come to Him in our poverty of spirit. This is what the writer of Hebrews meant when he encouraged us to "make every effort to enter that rest" (Hebrews 4:11). We will consider this again in the next chapter. But for now we need to see that we begin to rest in God when we cease to keep up fronts and pretenses with Him, as if God cannot see us in our core, as we truly are.

Our "rest" in God continues when we stand before Him in total honesty about our loves and hates, our desires and ambitions, and recognize that this is the daily exercise of our journey of spiritual growth in Christ. We begin by saying, "This is exactly who I am, what I want, and what I think *right now*. Train me how to become like You."

But how do we train? What is God's part in leading, coaching, teaching, empowering? What is our part in choosing to follow what He's teaching us, in responding to His work in a right spirit?

What we need to learn is how to *interact* with the grace of God, which is always at work in and around us. And that is where we turn our attention now.

CHAPTER THREE

THE GLORIOUS PURSUIT

> Grace, we must learn, is opposed to
> earning, not to effort.
>
> DALLAS WILLARD

> If godliness is not from deep within you, it is only a mask.
>
> JEANNE GUYON

—◄O►—

I MAGINE THAT ONE NIGHT GOD WAKES YOU FROM A DREAM AND offers you the golfing ability of Tiger Woods. That would be something, wouldn't it? Or imagine being bestowed with the computer or entrepreneurial capabilities of Bill Gates: "You can create the next Microsoft," God says. "Interested?"

Or maybe you're more the cultural type, and your heart would beat faster if God enabled you to sing like Pavarotti, to write like Jane Austen, or to paint like Rembrandt.

We could get lost all day in fantasies such as these, but in fact, reality for the Christian is much more stunning. Suppose God says, "You can have *My* eternal life in you."

The truth of Christianity is that God offers us something infinitely more valuable than all human abilities put together: According to the apostle Paul, we can have "the mind of Christ" (1 Corinthians 2:16).

Think about that for a minute. Somehow, spiritually, as Christians, we have the mind—that is the knowledge of God, the attitudes of heart—of Jesus, *God made man.*

This is an incredible offer. We are talking about a possibility that should take our breath away. We are being told that we can become like the greatest human being who ever lived.

This is a pursuit for the ages. Offered this opportunity, how could we ever settle for less? God is telling us that we can forsake the eternally inconsequential pursuits that consume our time, energy, and passion, and can adopt a new pursuit—spiritual growth in the character of Christ. It's bold. It's daring. It sounds unachievable, but the Bible promises that it's within our grasp: We can become like Christ.

But how?

THE DIVINE NATURE

Because of his astonishing failures, Peter often is characterized as sort of the thickheaded buffoon who always acted impetuously and who just didn't quite "get it." If the church spent as much time getting to know the Peter of the Epistles as the Peter of the Gospels, we would be struck by a profound understanding of the depth in spiritual growth I am talking about. Peter "grew up" in Christ and reached an understanding of faith that few attain. If we got to know *this* Peter, we wouldn't dare dismiss him as a hasty, comical disciple.

I'm convinced of this by Peter's second epistle in particular, which is a masterful call to spiritual growth. Peter began his letter by assuring the saints that God's "divine power has given us everything we need for life and godliness" (2 Peter 1:3). God, said Peter, gives us everything we need to live—not just to exist in body, but to *live!* He also has given us everything we need for godliness—in other words, everything we need to experience and become trained in the character of Christ.

Right away, this seems too good to be true. And then Peter upped the ante. He took us one step further by assuring us that through God's "precious promises" we "may participate in the divine nature and escape the corruption in the world caused by evil desires" (verse 4).

Peter did not say we *will* participate in the divine nature, but that we *may.* What might keep us back? Focusing on the wrong goal, to begin with. Let's look at some of the "false starts" that can lead us away.

DEAD-END PATHS

The first wrong path many of us take is the *recruiter* approach to the practice of Christianity. Many evangelicals make the mistake of thinking we have become saved basically so we can stay at the head of the spiritual path and recruit others. In this approach, we should know the Bible like a kid has memorized the back of a cereal box so that we have a potent arsenal with which to demolish every conceivable argument against the gospel. While evangelism is a glorious experience, the recruiter approach tends to reduce "partaking in the divine nature" to nothing *but* evangelism: We are saved by grace simply to see others be saved by grace.

There is also the end goal of *holiness*. Some Christians are taught that if they can somehow achieve "sinless perfection," they can finally please God. Every sin is viewed as a step back, which only time (and the work of Christ on the cross) can erase. The focus in this life is not experiencing the abundant life as much as it is avoiding the sinful life. Many Christians have made *their own righteousness* the end goal and have found that it makes them morbidly introspective and miserable.

Today, more and more people set their eyes on the goal of *activism*. This approach says, "As long as I sacrifice quantities of my time, live meagerly, and focus mainly on service to God, I'll be living a God-pleasing life . . . and hopefully, I'll be too busy to be selfish and sinful." For many of these people, stress and guilt and drivenness take their toll. Christlikeness, which results from entering the soul's sabbath rest, is lost.

Some more enterprising Christians have concocted the goal of *passivism*. Using logic as a shield rather than a sword, their argument goes something like this: Christ has already done everything on the cross. There's nothing I can do. God will change me; it's *all* up to Him. As long as I show up at church with respectful regularity, read my Bible, and pray when I really get in a bind, then God will make me into a brand-new person.

There is also a *pessimistic* approach that goes further, teaching Christians that they are lowly "worms" who are so depraved they never can rise above their sorry, sinful state. This approach errs on the side of man's fallenness, and it puts off our inheritance in Christ until a far future date, instead of recognizing that our glorious transformation is as much a part of our witness as our logical knowledge of the Bible — and it begins now.

There are several other approaches, but I will mention only one more: There are Christians who are waiting for a supernatural "lightning strike" from on high to *transform them in an instant*. The end goal for some, but not all, is to become conduits of this supernatural power. They are focused mainly on Jesus' miracle-working power, and very little on His humanity, character, or suffering.

Each one of these approaches, or paths, contains a grain of truth. It *is* important to share our faith with others. We *should* avoid sin. Our beliefs *will* result in service to God and society and other men. God *is* the primary change agent in our lives. We *can* experience a power that is beyond all human power.

But where each approach errs is in making an idol out of a single truth. When we insist on any one truth, we block the power and direction of other truths. And the problem with all these approaches is that they tend to focus on *how we can stay in favor, or prove our favor, with God*. These approaches to the Christian life are a galaxy away from the life modeled by Christ (and taught by His disciples), a life governed by an entire range of interior attitudes and orientations, which created the most beautiful and perfect life that has ever been lived. Our race is growth in the virtues of Christ. Our end goal is nothing less than Christlikeness.

THE REAL POWER IN OUR VEINS

A number of years ago, my oldest daughter became enthralled with the Olympic figure skaters. One night she asked me, "Now Papa, if you enter the Olympics, you get a gold, silver, or bras, right?"

I was in the middle of a book and eager to return to it, so I decided to overlook her faux pas.

"That's right, Allison," I mumbled.

"But little girls can't wear bras, can they?" she asked me in a worried voice.

And that's when I understood what was going on. My precious daughter was afraid that she would enter the Olympics, take third place, and receive an award for which she had absolutely no use.

I decided to respond on a literal level and said, "That's right, honey, little girls don't need to wear bras," at which Allison hiked up her shirt just over her stomach, looked down and said, "But I'm on my way, right?"

Allison understood that physical development is an inexorable and natural part of life. Her spiritual development, however, won't happen so easily or naturally. She'll have to *choose* to grow. And so do we.

Jesus' followers testified to a dynamic inner reality which resulted in outward growth: "Inwardly we are being renewed day by day" (2 Corinthians 4:16). But a conundrum soon presents itself, as many Christians well know. Read this next verse slowly, as Paul suggests something that at first glance sounds very strange: "To this end I labor, struggling with all *his* energy, which so powerfully works in me" (Colossians 1:29, emphasis added). Paul is laboring. But he is struggling with *God's* energy, not his own, "which so powerfully works" *within* him.

In the context of this particular passage, Paul is not directly addressing spiritual growth, but he is pointing to an underlying spiritual principle, one that is repeated several times throughout the New Testament: We are working, but doing so with a supernatural strength in us. A more explicit passage regarding spiritual growth is found in Philippians 2:12-13: "Continue to work out your salvation with fear and trembling, for it is God who works in you to will and to act according to his good purpose."

Many Christians have been hung up on these contradictions. Does God work, or do we work? Are we already perfect, or are we in the process of being made perfect?

The truth is, these realities are complementary, not contradictory. The small forces of our decision making, our will, and our mental and physical efforts need to connect with a force infinitely greater and eternally different from our own. They need to meet the limitless dynamism of God's will, power, and His efforts toward us. It's a process of choosing to cooperate, giving over our relatively minuscule powers of will and muscle, rather than canceling out the working of His grace in us.

The virtues are the key to understanding this. They provide the bridge between the forces of God's choice to empower and transform us and our choice to take the right attitudes about it. Apart from Christ, these qualities are lifeless cardboard replicas — an adaptation of the world's version of do's and dont's. But within the context of faith, these spiritual principles can literally reshape a life.

AN OLD PATH TO NEW LIFE

Though these ideas may seem new to some of us — and that in itself is unfortunate — the ancients clearly understood this "path" of Christian growth. John Climacus, who wrote a fifth-century classic of the Christian faith entitled *The Ladder of Divine Ascent,* assures us, "A [Christian] is shaped by virtues in the way that others are shaped by pleasures."[1]

If you approach the virtues as nothing more than obligations, you're going to labor without being able to rest. And unless you're carried along by God's power working within you, you'll be crushed by the seeming impossibility of spiritual growth. But as we progress, we come to understand how "contradictory" truths are really "complementary": In Christ we are already perfect as we are being made perfect; we labor with God's strength, not our own, and our labor is a constant struggle to stay at rest in God's acceptance and empowerment; and this allows a powerful dynamic to take place — an inner orientation will begin to carry us along so that what once seemed like labor becomes the cherished inner passion that drives our life.

Here are two analogies that may help this make sense.

My oldest brother came to visit our house when we lived in Virginia, and, as we sat in the back yard one day, he looked at our flowerbeds and said, "I think I'm going to do some weeding."

I thought he was crazy. Here he was, on vacation, wanting to work in our flowerbeds. But to him it wasn't work; it just looked like work *to me.* To my brother, this was a restful thing to do, and he really enjoyed it.

Personally, I feel the same deep satisfaction when I run. I'm sweating, my heart is beating fast, but I'm loving it. It looks like work to those who watch me from the outside, but if they could see the inner reality, they'd see I'm deriving satisfaction from the effort.

When God re-creates us, what looks like "work" to the outside world becomes a delightful "rest." We're loving it, even as we're sweating. Why? A dynamic change has occurred within us. We cherish the spiritual freedom created by each virtue as it begins to blossom; we experience the power of a transformed life, and we're drawn to want more of godliness in the same way we used to be drawn to plunge deeper into sin.

Throw any pleasure in front of a hedonist, and he can't resist. He's captivated by its imprisoning force. Dangle a virtue in front of a healthy Christian, and her heart is liberated to walk in that light. She's enchanted by it, can't wait to revel in it, and runs after it accordingly. This is what Jesus was talking about when He said, "Blessed are those who *hunger and thirst* for righteousness, for they will be filled" (Matthew 5:6, emphasis added). In *The Message,* Eugene Peterson phrases it this way: "You're blessed when you've worked up a good appetite for God. He's food and drink in the best meal you'll ever eat."

To an immature kid, eating dinner can be a chore: "I don't like peas! Fish? Are you kidding me? You want me to eat fish?" But to a mature adult, eating can be a real pleasure. The difference isn't in the activity—the man is eating the same food he rejected as a boy—but his *orientation* has completely changed. He has matured.

If we don't sense this inner orientation toward righteousness, it simply means our souls are unrefined and pre-adolescent, spiritually speaking. We might still be on our way to heaven, but we're still far too weighed down by the world.

FEEDING THE SOUL FOR HEALTHY GROWTH

But *why* do we need to grow? Peter provides us with some sobering words. After telling us that we can participate in the divine nature, he dared to say, "For this very reason, make *every effort* to add to your faith goodness" (2 Peter 1:5, emphasis added). After listing spiritual qualities in which we should grow—knowledge, self-control, perseverance, godliness, brotherly kindness, love, and so on—Peter explained, "For if you possess these qualities in increasing measure, they will keep you from being ineffective and unproductive in your knowledge of our Lord Jesus Christ" (verse 8).

Peter never said we add to our faith *to be saved.* But he did point out that if we don't add to our faith, we'll be *ineffective* and *unproductive,* and our knowledge of the Lord Jesus Christ will not result in much change. That's the important distinction, which Christians of the past understood. As the great Calvinist writer, John Owen, wrote, "God works in us and with us, not against us or without us."[2]

The warning imbedded in Peter's verse is this: You and I can *know* the way to transformation but actually miss experiencing it on a personal level. We can live this entire life "saved" but relatively unchanged. That's tragic because, if we do not "partake" in the divine nature of Christ, we can starve our soul until it is limp and powerless. For our sake, Peter urged us to make *every effort.*

In *The Screwtape Letters,* C. S. Lewis has the mentor demon, Screwtape, encourage Wormwood after a seemingly devastating setback. Even though Wormwood's man has become a Christian, Screwtape reminds him there is yet a sliver of hope: "I note with grave displeasure that your patient has become a Christian. . . . There is no need to despair. . . . All the *habits* of the patient, both mental and bodily, are still in our favor."[3]

Though the eternal penalty for old "habits" is completely removed upon salvation, these habits have a pesky way of hanging around to pester us, like a small dog that runs when we yell at it but circles back and attacks from behind the second our backs are turned. We practice and grow in the virtues of Christ and let His nature feed us in order to create new habits of holiness. We press forward to grow in His attributes not out of fear, but because growing in His character is the path we travel to maintain intimacy with the Lover and Lord of our soul.

If we do not grow in grace and spirit, those of us who are serious about our faith are likely to be lured by legalism or at least by the tendency to measure ourselves against other people. We need to know what we can aspire *to,* rather than becoming obsessed with what we must fight to avoid. Legalists and perfectionists focus on the "cant's": "I can't do this; I mustn't do that."

Taking off sin *is* an important component of Christian spiritual growth, but it's only the first step. After we take off, we need to "put on."

The clearest Scriptures on Christian growth are in Ephesians: "You were taught, with regard to your former way of life, to put off your old self, which is being corrupted by its deceitful desires; to be made new in the attitude of your minds; *and to put on the new self,* created to be like God in true righteousness and holiness" (4:22-24, emphasis added).

Many of us know we cannot escape an old habit, or a pattern of sin, by focusing on it and trying hard to avoid it. Before we know it we've become sin-focused, and the energy we invest in trying to stop has the effect of a tire spinning in mud: Somehow we entrench ourselves deeper into the very act we're trying to stop. That's why any discussion of Christian growth apart from growth in the spiritual virtues is incomplete, maybe even detrimental. The virtues tell us what to put on—the attributes of Jesus. They sculpt the future and provide a much more healthy focus.

Clothing ourselves in Christ is the lifelong process, then, by which we put off the old and put on the new.

COOPERATING CHRISTIANS

Can you taste this invitation of a new life in Christ? Are you eager to get your life back? Before we get into the individual virtues, let's briefly explore three qualities of a person who is cooperating with God.

First, a "cooperating Christian" has an earnestness about his growth. Consider this earnestness the "invitation," the opening up of our soul to God's holy light. Jonathan Edwards, the great eighteenth-century pastor and revivalist, wrote, "The religion which God requires and will accept does not consist of weak, dull, and lifeless wishes which scarcely raise us above indifference. In His Word, God insists that we be 'fervent' in spirit and *actively engage our hearts . . .* (Romans 12:11)."[4]

Step out of your shoes and imagine this from God's perspective: He offers us the most glorious, fulfilling, and meaningful pursuit possible in human experience, and by our lethargic reactions, we say, "Well, okay, maybe—unless something better comes up." The Bible is very frank in this regard. When people casually reject God's initiative and invitation, He gets angry, and he moves on, inviting others (see Matthew 22).

Remember, Jesus said only those who *hunger and thirst* after righteousness will be filled. Many of us experience indifference, either because we do not care or do not know about the power of grace that is available to us for growth and change. But the hunger for righteousness is also the hunger to become the mature, responsible people we wish to be.

As Edwards said, "The Scriptures often represent the search, effort, and labor that occur in a Christian chiefly *after* his conversion.

Yet his conversion is only the beginning of his work. From then [the Christian] has to stand, press forward, reach out. . . . "[5]

Even though this calling is so glorious, many of us take it for granted. If our priorities were straight, we'd see this disinterest as scandalous: "We are nothing if we are not in earnest about our faith, and if our wills and inclinations are not intensely exercised. The religious life contains things too great for us to be lukewarm."[6]

The second characteristic of a cooperating Christian is streamlined living. If our lives are consumed by secondary pursuits, we'll never be able to grasp the one, most important pursuit—new life in Christ. Edwards said a Christian is someone who "places holy living above everything else. This is his main preoccupation; he is devoted to it with the greatest diligence and earnestness."[7]

Baseball's "iron man," Cal Ripken Jr., has credited part of his phenomenal success to his early, streamlined focus. While other neighborhood kids wanted to be good at all sports, Cal clung to baseball—and look at the result.

The third characteristic of a cooperating Christian is a restful and passionate relationship with God. If we pursue holiness *ahead* of or apart from Christ, "trying hard" will either burn us out or tempt us into hypocrisy. Delight in God's love and His plan to give you your life back. Revel in it, and let the desire to grow and experience such a freedom motivate you from within. Though this isn't an easy process, it can be a delightful one.

We're now going to enter a new section in this book, in which we explore the concrete virtues that will help you claim your true inheritance, enabling you to become a partaker in the divine nature as you escape the corruptions of this world. Each one of these virtues represents a doorway through which you can travel to overcome your "God resistance" and enter into a new understanding of who God is. Each virtue represents a window you can open to your soul, thereby transforming you as you begin to experience Christ.

Let's start opening those windows.

SECTION TWO
THE CLASSICAL VIRTUES

CHAPTER FOUR

LIVING WHERE YOU ARE
(HUMILITY, PART ONE)

Saints agree they are sinners;
only sinners think they are saints.

PETER KREEFT

The truth is this—pride must die in you,
or nothing of heaven can live in you.

ANDREW MURRAY

◄○►

"SO HOW'D YOUR MORNING WORK GO?" MY WIFE, LISA, ASKED ME. "I lost a good bit of it. My computer crashed."

She looked at me with astonishment. "I can't believe you're taking it so well."

I shrugged. "I've written by hand and I've written on computers. Over the long run, computers have saved me a lot of time. I can't complain if they take a little time back now and then."

"But your *attitude*," Lisa said. "I think I'd be furious."

As Lisa left the room, I thought, *She's right. I do have a really good attitude. I like that. Instead of ranting and raving, I just accept it and move on. That's good. That's mature. That's how Christ would respond.*

Later that same day, my kids didn't do what they were supposed to do. Lisa became . . . upset. A little later, I forgot to do something I was supposed to do. Lisa became upset again.

I began to judge her. *I have this great attitude,* I told myself, *but Lisa's is awful. Why can't she roll with the punches like I do?*

Being the one with the mature attitude, I felt it was my duty to lecture her on how rotten hers had become.

Later that evening, God zeroed in on my pride. I saw how I had let Lisa's compliment go to my head. As soon as pride was conceived, I became a judge. In the morning, I might have had a Christlike attitude; by the evening, I'd become a Pharisee.

Pride is that potent, that destructive, that abusive, and that offensive. Relationally, there are few things so obnoxious as self-righteousness. Spiritually, there are few things so injurious or even lethal as pride.

The irony is, the more we experience the character of Christ, the more natural reason we'll have to become prideful. John Climacus warns us to "rebuff the vanity that follows obedience."[1] If we're not careful, spiritual growth can sabotage itself. Maybe that's why you cannot read far in the Christian classics without having people testify to the absolute necessity and foundation of humility.

John Calvin calls humility the "sovereign virtue . . . the mother and root of all virtue."[2] Edwards agrees, calling humility the "most essential thing in true religion."[3]

Andrew Murray calls humility the "root" of our spiritual life. If we lack this root, he insists, we lack the vibrancy of the Christian life as God intends it. "Is it any wonder that the Christian life is so often feeble and fruitless, when the very root of the Christ-life is neglected, is unknown? Is it any wonder that the joy of salvation is so little felt, when that in which Christ found it and brings it is so little sought? We must seek a humility which will rest in nothing less than the end and death of self."[4]

In all of our discipleship, we teach prayer, we teach Bible study, and we teach evangelism. These are necessary disciplines. But without the interior foundation of humility, they can't possibly support our spiritual house. To experience the life of Christ, we need the *inner* discipline of humility. If you've attempted to build a spiritual life from the outside in, bypassing humility, you probably feel tired, disillusioned, frustrated, or just plain lifeless. The solution isn't to neglect the outer disciplines, it's to begin practicing the inner disciplines as well, beginning with Christ's foundational attitude of humility.

If the Christian classics agree that humility is the most important starting point for the Christian life, why do we so neglect the interior life? Why are most of us taught how to do everything *except* cultivate this most important inner virtue?

Perhaps it's because the inner disciplines and virtues are so diffi-cult to teach and model. I can check off a completed Bible study, record my minutes in prayer, or write down the names of the people with whom I share my faith. But how do I check off the attainment of humility?

I can't. The truth is this: *We don't become humble as much as we learn to practice humility.* The virtues aren't a state of being as much as they are inner disciplines after which we aspire. We enter into the virtues by degrees, and perhaps nowhere is this as true as it is with the virtue of humility.

Teaching and modeling the outer disciplines without the inner dis-ciplines inevitably creates gifted but empty and proud Christians. Let's begin to recapture the ancient and fundamental discipline of humility by examining how Scripture and the Christian classics define it.

RADICAL GOD-DEPENDENCE

Have you ever met a Christian who seems to do everything right, who always knows the right things to say, who has admirable levels of dis-cipline, but who just seems to lack the *spirit* of Christ? Maybe you couldn't put your finger on it, but you sensed that while everything was right on the outside, something profoundly important was miss-ing on the inside. Most often, this "something" is the spirit of Christ—humility. The most carefully groomed outer life can't com-pletely mask the ugliness of pride that lurks within.

From a spiritual perspective, humility is entering into the life of Christ through a radical God-dependence. It's an inner orientation of actively receiving from God and acknowledging our need. The humble Christian is the Christian who takes literally Christ's words: "Apart from me you can do nothing."[5] Andrew Murray nails humility exactly when he calls it "the displacement of self by the enthronement of God."[6]

Calvin goes so far as to voice his agreement with Augustine that humility is not evidenced simply when "a man, aware that he has some virtues, abstains from pride and arrogance; but when man feels that he has no refuge except in humility."[7]

What do Calvin and Augustine mean, that a Christian can find absolutely no refuge except in humility? They mean that the Christian has shifted from a human-centered faith to a God-centered faith; that the root, fruit, and maintenance of his walk is dependent on God's work, God's favor, and God's strength. He not only knows this, he acknowledges this and lives by this in a practical way.

Humility is the disposition that makes us available to be blessed by God. The Psalms seem obsessed with God's eagerness to reach out to the humble: God saves the humble,[8] guides the humble,[9] sustains the humble,[10] and even crowns the humble.[11] Notice that everything flows *from* God *to* the humble servant.

Pride seeks to reverse this. Pride is self-reliance and self-dependence. Arrogance seeks to *obligate* God instead of *receive* from Him.

In college, I asked a nonbeliever to come with me to a John Fisher concert. In the seventies and early eighties, John's thoughtful and informed lyrics made him one of my favorite contemporary Christian musicians. I was confident that John would present the gospel in a mature way. He did. John gave a particularly challenging invitation after singing a song about being a beggar telling other beggars where he found bread.

I eagerly awaited my friend's response but was immediately disappointed.

"I'm not a beggar," he insisted. "When I come to God, I'm going to come bringing Him something, not asking for His help."

This pride kept him from entering the spiritual life. The same pride keeps many of us from *growing* in the spiritual life. Some of us think that after we receive God's salvation, then everything is up to us. This self-dependence cuts off our "spiritual oxygen." We're virtually paralyzed until we learn to breathe the fresh air of God's empowerment, grace, and assistance.

FORGETTING SELF

We've been talking about what humility looks like between us and God, but humility toward our neighbor is just as important. Paul tells us to "show true humility toward all men."[12] What does this humility look like?

At the heart of "social" humility is self-forgetfulness. So often, we live as if the primary calling of the world and everyone around us is to make us happy, healthy, comfortable, and affluent. If anyone or anything dares to get in the way of this ultimate aim, we erupt into anger, resentment, and bitterness. Who cares if our waiter is having a bad day; we want our dinner!

A friend of mine from seminary faced this dilemma. He was cramming for an ethics final when he got a knock on the door. His inebriated neighbor needed to be taken to detox. His initial thought was, *I can't spend two hours taking some drunk to detox; I have to study for my social ethics class!* When he realized the irony of what he was thinking, he put on his coat, picked up his car keys, and placed another person first.

The world doesn't revolve around any one of us, and the demand that it should do so creates nothing but frustration. There's no good time to have a family crisis; it's *never* convenient to get a flat tire. The inner discipline of humility acts like a filter, saving us from the tyranny of grossly unrealistic expectations that everyone and everything should bend our way.

Self-forgetfulness also means we are liberated to serve others at God's direction, rather than trying to impress them. The ultimate picture of this is Jesus, washing the feet of His disciples.[13]

The lust to be served, honored, and noticed is nothing less than the lust to be treated like God. This monumental arrogance never can be satisfied; we will never become God. That's why pride always leaves the aftertaste of frustration. Humility, on the other hand, can never be disappointed; if you want to serve someone, you can always find someone to serve — and in doing so, you'll experience the joy and fulfillment of Christ.

Which life would you rather have? One in which your expectations will never be met and which leaves behind frustration and despair, or one that ushers in the very presence of Christ? Do you sense the churning of frustrated pride in your life? Do you need the inner discipline of humility?

It is important to be very clear in what we mean when we use the word "humility." Some well-meaning but misguided Christians have tried artificially to manufacture the humble spirit and ended up creating a new form of pride.

SELF-OBSESSED BIAS

"John" was one of the most frustrating Christians I've ever worked with. He was passionately committed to following the Lord, but his conscience tyrannized him. He became obsessed with how sinful he was, and he couldn't pray for ten minutes without falling into despair about his spiritual bankruptcy.

The irony is, contrary to popular opinion, John wasn't humble. Merely thinking ill of ourselves is not a healthy spiritual exercise. As Kreeft points out, "Humility is thinking less *about* yourself, not thinking less *of* yourself."[14]

John's obsession with his own weaknesses meant that he was still the center of his own attention. He focused on his sinfulness instead of his strength, but from a Christian perspective, any obsession with the self still is considered pride.

Other Christians think that humility means denying what we know to be true with falsely self-deprecating statements: "I'm not *really* a good businessman; my success is mostly due to luck"; "Actually, I'm a very poor student, even though I get straight As." Being humble doesn't mean pretending we don't have gifts; Jesus never pretended that He wasn't the Son of God.

Instead of leading us into denial, humility leads us into using our gifts to *serve* rather than to *impress*. It changes the inner reality and attitude with which we view the talents that God has given us. "Jesus knew that the Father had put all things under his power," *so* He started to wash the disciples' feet.[15]

When people try to prove themselves by their gifts instead of serving people with their gifts, they shrink their lives. They become incapable of taking equal enjoyment and delight in the accomplishments of others. They don't want to be a good or faithful singer, pastor, preacher, parent, entrepreneur, or Christian, they want to be the *best*. So they cringe when others do well. Life becomes a competition. Humility is the inner attitude and discipline that sets us free from this self-obsessed bias.

In *The Screwtape Letters,* Screwtape explains, "[God] wants [the Christian], in the end, to be so free from any bias in his own favor that he can rejoice in his own talents as frankly and gratefully as in his neighbor's talents—or in a sunrise, an elephant, or a waterfall. He wants each man, in the long run, to be able to recognize all creatures (even himself) as glorious and excellent things. He wants to kill their animal self-love as soon as possible."[16]

If I'm a humble parent, I can clap loudly, enthusiastically, and sincerely when my friend's kid wins a scholarship, even if my child barely managed to graduate. If I'm a humble neighbor, I can genuinely rejoice when someone from my street is finally able to afford a five-acre lot, even if my back yard is the size of a postage stamp.

The humble life is a life in which deep joy and profound appreciation become a daily occurrence because the wellspring of that joy isn't limited solely to our own personal good fortune. We can appreciate others without feeling diminished because they have skills we don't; we can revel in the beauty of a landscape without feeling envious that we don't own it; we can be fed by a well-preached sermon rather than fretting over the fact that we're not behind the pulpit.

Selfless living is liberated living. It recaptures the present, enabling us to live for today without letting our thirst for more destroy our present enjoyment. Rather than lust for more money, more power, or more recognition, we can wait for God. Peter wrote, "Humble yourselves, therefore, under God's mighty hand, that *he may lift you up in due time.*"[17] When we become content to live in the present, God has given us our lives back in a vivid way; we no longer destroy the present by looking for a better future or a more celebrated now. We are set free to live the life that God created uniquely for us.

LIVING YOUR LIFE

A few years ago, the commercials sang, "I want to be like Mike." As playground kids danced to the jingle, Michael Jordan soared across a basketball court, flying into a brilliant leaping dunk. "I want to be like Mike," the kids sang over and over.

The tragedy is that commercials like these are pushing our children into "vicarious" living. Rather than seeking their own destinies, they settle for living in the shadow of someone else. Millions of kids (including my own) wear shirts with athletes' names on the back.

God has given each one of us a life that He has given to no one else. We have our own character, skills, and body. Humility helps us accept an honest assessment of who we are, while daydreams about being someone else or someone better do nothing but make us spiritually hungry. Humility leads us to personal fulfillment rather than to fantasy and denial.

You see, pride can lead us to reach higher than God enabled us to reach. And pride can sometimes lead us to set our sights lower than we should, simply because we're afraid to try and possibly fail; that would be too much for our egos to take. The same humility that cuts through the buzz of blind ambition also cuts through the paralyzing fear of failure. Humility gives us unparalleled fulfillment in completing the task specifically ordained for us.

I have a good friend who, in college, would never have been labeled humble. If anything, he was seen as cocky and arrogant. But God called him to be an associate pastor, a position he filled for almost fifteen years, until his mid-thirties. I never would have imagined this man willingly working as the "number two" guy in a church for that long. I always thought he'd need to be the senior pastor, but he learned to practice humility and found great joy in the place where God called him to be.

Another college friend of mine was working as an associate pastor, something most of his friends expected. Then the church he was with encouraged him to plant a sister church in a neighboring community. He became a senior pastor, something that surprised us all. We couldn't see him as the main leader of a church. He didn't seem to have the disposition or drive. But in humility, my friend accepted that calling, and in humility, he's living it out. He doesn't pretend to have it all together. He knows there are areas where he needs help, but he also realizes it would be arrogant for anyone to try to be a pastor on his own. His sense of need makes him a much stronger pastor.

In my own life, humility helps preserve the integrity of my vocational life. I'm not an "A-list" writer or a household name. You probably didn't buy this book because you had heard of me, but because the subject interested you. Accordingly, I often take side work as a "ghostwriter" (or unnamed co-author) to pay the bills. I'll interview someone and tell his story for him. During this process, some great lines will pop into my head in the process of writing. Inevitably, I'll pause. *I should save that line for one of my own books!* I'll think. *That's a good one!*

But always God reminds me of my calling. He lets me know that the river of His kingdom needs to flow freely without every individual Christian building a dam with his name on it to let everyone know, "This work of God passed through me first!"

If everything good has been birthed in God, what does it matter whose hands it has passed through? We are simply the mail carriers, not the writers. Would your mail carrier stand outside your door and shout, "I just want you to know, I delivered this Christmas card! You wouldn't have received it if I hadn't been faithful to put it in your box"? Yet in Christian circles, too many of us cling tenaciously to each distinguishing mark of God's grace and favor. We erect dams every ten inches so we can "control" what God has given to us.

We do this because we have finite minds that haven't grasped the unlimited bounty of an infinite God. Am I to believe that God can only entrust me with so many "good lines"? Is God's Spirit—which passionately desires to speak truth to God's people—running out of powerful analogies?

When we slip from the foundation of a "giving life" to the cavern of a "notice-me life," we live in a state of high frustration. Ambition grinds up people. To embrace humility is to be liberated from the insatiable search for self-significance.

Humility will become a passion for us when we realize that the more we put our own egos out of the way, the more the life and power and purpose of God can pass through us. When this happens, something glorious takes place: We get to experience the quality of eternal life without the taint of our own control and small ego demands.

Since humility is so important—the queen of the virtues—we need to give closer attention to it in the next chapter, to look at how we lay the foundation of Christlike living by practicing this inner discipline.

CHAPTER FIVE

THE BEAUTIFUL SPIRIT
(HUMILITY, PART TWO)

Humility is the bloom and the beauty of holiness.
ANDREW MURRAY

*Unless we make the increase of humility our study, we
may find that we have been delighting in beautiful thoughts
and feelings, in solemn acts of consecration and faith, while the only
sure mark of the presence of God — the disappearance of self —
was all the time wanting.*
ANDREW MURRAY

◄O►

FOLLOWING THE STUNNING VICTORY AT YORKTOWN, THE AMERI-
can colonies seemed determined to clutch defeat out of the jaws of
victory. Many assumed the Revolutionary War was over, but since
George Washington was well aware that the British forces on North
American soil still outnumbered the Continental Army, the American
soldiers weren't let go. The soldiers weren't well paid or well taken care
of, and given plenty of time to sit, they started to fret. Washington soon
realized that the biggest threat to morale was idleness.

To make matters worse, the Continental Congress cut expenses by
reducing the number of regiments and reneging on back pay. The fury
this aroused became truly perilous. Even high-ranking officers spoke
of taking the law into their own hands. It was obvious that they'd
risked their lives . . . only to be sent home in poverty as soon as they
weren't needed.

As usually happens in revolutions, top leadership in the army
realized that with a weak, fledgling central government, they held the

real power. There was only one man standing in their way: George Washington.

In what historian James Thomas Flexner calls "probably the most important single gathering ever held in the United States,"[1] Washington had to face the wrath of his own officers. The contentious meeting took place on March 15, 1783. Washington spoke of his self-less service, his love for his country and his soldiers, and his confidence that in the end, the government would act appropriately. He begged his men not to destroy their own new nation.

But when his prepared speech was finished, Washington saw that these war-toughened officers were unmoved. His heart must have gone cold, realizing that anarchy was about to swallow the nascent states.

Perhaps fearful of sitting down and letting the unpersuaded mob go free, according to Flexner, Washington reached for a "reassuring" letter from a congressman. Could a statesman's words reach them where a general's had failed? Flexner recounts:

"[Washington] pulled the paper from his pocket, and then something seemed to go wrong. The General seemed confused; he stared at the paper helplessly. The officers leaned forward, their hearts contracting with anxiety. Washington pulled from his pocket something only his intimates had ever seen him wear: a pair of eyeglasses. 'Gentlemen,' he said, 'you will permit me to put on my spectacles, for I have not only grown gray but almost blind in the service of my country.'

"This homely act and simple statement did what all Washington's arguments had failed to do. The hardened soldiers wept. Washington had saved the United States from tyranny and civil discord."

Later, Thomas Jefferson would reflect on this incident and comment: "The moderation and virtue of a single character probably prevented this Revolution from being closed, as most others have been. . . ."[2]

In Jefferson's own words, virtue saved the United States. A display of humility accomplished what words could not. Where Washington's rhetoric was found wanting, his weak eyes proved decisive, and men's hearts were won.

There is power in humility, power when we shun the arrogance of the world and meet one another in an entirely new dimension.

SPIRITUAL CLOTHING

On my wedding day, I thought I should do my best to look "extra nice," but after thirty minutes of preparation, I didn't know what else to do. I had shaved, showered, combed my hair, even trimmed my fingernails. Yet I knew that Lisa had allotted the entire morning to "get ready." Stumped as to what should be my next hygienic move, I simply resolved to sit down and try not to wrinkle my tux.

And then when I saw my bride, dressed in her flowing gown, her teeth a dazzling white, well . . . I still didn't know all that she had done for the past four hours, but I sure liked the result.

In the same way, Peter calls us to dress ourselves spiritually. He urges us, "Clothe yourselves with humility."[3] Taking on this character trait of Christ is how we become beautiful to God. And it is how God begins to become a beautiful presence in our lives.

Re-outfitting your inner man with humility is an ongoing process, but there are a few tried-and-true practices which Christians have used to train themselves in this attitude of Christ:

1. Change your focus

According to the Scriptures, humility is born in the soul that is overwhelmed by the experience and knowledge of God.[4] This is the first step to practicing humility—switching our focus from ourselves to the grandeur of God's greatness.

Edwards distinguishes between what he calls "legal humiliation" and "evangelical humiliation." Legal humiliation leads us to a sense of smallness and self-abasement—what my friend John suffered from—but evangelical humiliation leads us to become overwhelmed by God's holy beauty.[5] Many of us have not escaped legalistic humiliation.

The scourge of legalistic humiliation is that it still focuses on the self; instead of bragging, the person caught in legalistic humility is obsessed with failure and shortcomings. But that's still a self-centered view, and it no more mirrors the spirit of Christ than does someone clothed in arrogance. Evangelical humiliation leads us to leave our strengths *and* weaknesses in the hands of God. Remember—humility is not a positive or negative view of self as much as it is a *forgetfulness* of self.

The surest road to humility is a constant remembrance of God. Scripturally, pride is connected with God-forgetfulness: "They became proud; then they forgot me."[6] When we don't take time to dwell on the power, beauty, holiness, awesomeness, and majesty of God, humility becomes a stranger, and pride becomes a raging force.

If you want to practice humility, learn how to remember God. Memorize some verses that remind you of His beauty; sing a hymn instead of turning on the radio as you drive down the road. When you wake up in the middle of the night and can't get back to sleep, meditate on Christ washing the feet of His disciples or submitting His body to the cross. Look up to the mountains or out to the heavens and think about the power of a Creator who could make such sights. Whatever it takes, create habits, rituals, and practices to intentionally remember God.

2. Adopt a posture of receiving

When I think of Christ, I think of Him as a pretty capable guy, but listen to His self-testimony: "The Son can do nothing by himself."[7] "My teaching is not my own. It comes from him who sent me."[8] "I do nothing on my own but speak just what the Father has taught me."[9] If *Jesus* had this attitude, how much more should we!

Adopting an attitude of receiving has been an incredibly liberating experience for me. Any number of times I've felt that I was in over my head, that I was being called to do something for which I had neither the ability nor the spirit. Instead of pretending otherwise, I simply confessed the truth to God: "I don't know what to do; I'm not up to this, and I need Your help." Without fail, He stepped in and met my lack with His provision.

It's okay to say, "God, I feel too weak and confused to be a good parent in this situation. I don't know what to do, and I need Your guidance." "Father, I've really blown this relationship. Can You help me set it right?" "Lord, I'm afraid to pray. It's so difficult. Will You help me?"

When I feel I have to prove myself to God, I have stepped outside of my rest in Him. Practically, this means that sometimes I can't immediately discipline my children or try to immediately reconcile a relationship. I might have to think about it, pray about it, maybe talk to others about it. I have to admit, "I need a better sense of direction; I can't act right now."

3. Expect growth through experience

The third element that builds humility is personal experience. James Ryle wrote, "The older you grow, and the more you see, the less reason you will find for being proud. Ignorance and inexperience are the pedestal of pride; once let the pedestal be removed, and pride will soon come tumbling down."[10]

Humility comes as we grow in experience, not just head knowledge. Not long ago, one of my commitments was at a conference that featured Dr. Jack Hayford as the keynote speaker. I listened as Dr. Hayford opened the talk with a couple of jokes. I've gained quite a bit of insight from this man's teaching and was surprised at what I considered a slow opening. Secretly, I had the audacity to compare it with my own opening earlier in the day. My talk fared better, of course.

Then Dr. Hayford delivered one of the most insightful, liberating, and powerful sermons I have ever heard. When he was done, I looked at the people sitting around me, and *all* our mouths were dropped open in astonishment. I'm not exaggerating this—he had touched our souls for God that deeply.

That evening, going back to my hotel room, I didn't have to work at humility. It was all around me. Above all, Dr. Hayford's wisdom, gained by a life of submission to God, reminded me I have a lot of growing to do.

4. Adopt a self-emptying spirit

On the heels of this, I need to say that time alone doesn't *guarantee* maturity. Neither does raw experience. Both can lead to arrogance rather than humility. What nurtures a humble heart is time and experience with God *while adopting a self-emptying spirit.*

This spirit begins in prayer. Pause for a moment and think about what characterized your most recent prayers. Did you approach God in humility? Is it possible that there may have been some pride, a lack of awareness concerning the holy nature of God and your own humble estate?

Jeanne Guyon provides a very practical primer on experiencing humility in prayer: "As you come to Him, come as a weak child, one who is all soiled and badly bruised—a child that has been hurt from falling again and again. Come to the Lord as one who has no strength of his own; come to Him as one who has no power to cleanse himself. Humbly lay your pitiful condition before your Father's gaze."[11]

Listen carefully to your own prayers. Do you approach God with secret annoyance—as if He's apathetic while you are the one who is truly concerned? Do you believe that God is less compassionate than you are? Listen to the spirit behind the prayers.

When we pray out of our spiritual poverty, we are adding our voice to a mighty chorus that has been prayed for centuries. The most mature souls have sought God with this spirit. The deepest writers, beginning with Isaiah, have understood the depths of our weakness: "All of us have become like one who is unclean, and all our righteous acts are like filthy rags."[12]

Adopting a self-emptying spirit means admitting that there is no way, *absolutely none,* that we can ever display humility unless God takes pity on us and imparts His own Spirit to transform us from within.

5. Practice humility toward others

Next—here's the truly difficult part—we learn to practice humility by displaying it before others with selfless living. Murray writes, "The insignificances of daily life are the . . . tests of eternity because they prove what spirit really possesses us. It is in our most unguarded moments that we really show and see what we are. To know . . . how the humble man behaves, you must follow him in the common course of daily life."[13]

Very recently, my family spent the night at a friend's house to celebrate New Year's Eve. I flew into town that day from the Midwest, so my "body clock" was already two hours ahead of everyone else's. When midnight rolled around, I was exhausted.

In the middle of the night, our friend came into our room and whispered, "Lisa!"

I was awake and guessed what was coming.

"Graham's feeling sick. He needs you."

Lisa started stirring. And I had a decision to make. I could pretend

I was asleep. After all, the woman was addressing my wife, not me. Besides, I had been up for almost twenty hours. It would be so easy just to close my eyes, but . . . was that the response of a servant?

"I'll take care of it," I said.

It was such an insignificant occurrence that I'm almost embarrassed to mention it. But humility is learned through such small decisions. I know I will never *become* humble, as a permanent state, but I need to learn to *practice* humility, and that can only be done through the routine, small acts of life in which I put others first.

6. Develop a healthy self-doubt

A healthy self-doubt is a wonderful thing. We should not set out to destroy a reasonable self-confidence, leading us to become insecure and indecisive. But practicing humility means we become open to considering the fact that there is almost always another angle we're missing.

In a dispute, for instance, humility can teach us not to assume that the other person is wrong just because he disagrees with us. And in fact, whether he is right or wrong is only one issue. Do we value him enough to listen to him, his doubts, questions, and misinformation, so we can gently correct his view? Do we slow down, let passions subside, and then try to see the situation from his perspective? Or do we demolish his opinion?

A healthy self-doubt redirects our judgments. We stop labeling, start listening, and take others into account. What if a mother started evaluating her own life as meticulously as she has fallen into evaluating her daughter's? What if a dissatisfied man focused on how he was failing as a husband instead of how his spouse was failing as a wife? What if a teenager quit complaining about how his parents have messed him up and started asking himself how he has neglected the command to honor them? What if a pastor focused on how he could serve his small church instead of how his church could fulfill his ambitions?

These are the prophetic calls of humility. They disarm our pride, redirect our focus, and lead us into selfless service to others.

Since practicing humility in relationships is such a crucial yet difficult discipline, let's take some time to look at this more closely.

THE MOTHER OF LOVE

Shortly after seminary, I was hired into a Christian ministry and soon came to verbal blows with an old college acquaintance who was then my immediate superior. I saw all his faults and resented his success. I didn't *covet* his success—I had no interest in doing what he was doing—but it bothered me that someone with such faults should be allowed such a platform. I became obsessed with his failings, and he understandably became wary of me. When somebody is judging you, it's difficult not to see him as a threat.

I thought it was my duty to bring my observations to the overall leader. My judgments weren't without some basis, and eventually the leader had to make a choice. In the end, he kept me on and my former superior was let go.

The relationship was almost irretrievably broken. Because many of my observations were correct and were backed up by others, I was smug in my self-righteousness and blinded to my pride for many years. Instead of stepping back and letting things move at their own pace, I proudly took everything into my own hands and destroyed a relationship.

While pride is the father of hate and dissension, humility is the mother of love and unity. Without humility, we become thoroughly disagreeable and demanding characters. John of the Cross tells us, "From this humility stems love of neighbor, for [we] will esteem them and not judge them."[14]

Estrangement, hate, anger, bitterness, and resentment, the killers of human relationships, are born in judgment. That's why John says humility is essential for us to love our neighbor. Where I've failed in humility, I've also failed in love.

My most meaningful relationships are ones with mutual respect. Think about somebody with whom you just cannot get along. If you're honest, somewhere down the line you've judged him. You haven't esteemed him very highly; in fact, you have elevated yourself over him. Maybe he *was* wrong, but were you *absolutely* right? You may have *different* faults, but you have faults nonetheless.

If ever there was proof of declining humility within the church and society, it's seen in the nature of our relationships and how we approach them. Years ago, I finally realized that marriage is for holiness more than happiness. For me, marriage creates the best environment in which I can serve God and grow in the character of Christ, and that's the greatest thing I should expect from it.

Once I understood this, the nature of marriage underwent a distinctly radical shift in my mind. When I was married for happiness, and I went through the inevitable seasons of unhappiness (or just the routines of life), I assumed my lack of happiness meant Lisa wasn't measuring up. I judged her failings, and she judged mine.

When I realized I was married for holiness, *I* never measured up, and I became more than satisfied with my wife as I focused on what *I* needed to change. My growth was not dependent on Lisa changing, but on my change in attitude and perspective.

What is divorce but millions of spouses saying, "You're not good enough for me"? This lack of humility is destroying our families and lives.

The beauty of humility is that we become empowered to respect others. Relationships are based on entering into other people's lives, but when we're so focused on ourselves, it is impossible to empty ourselves enough to care about someone else. "The humble man looks upon every child of God—even the feeblest and unworthiest—and honors him and prefers him in honor as the son of a King."[15]

God wants to give us our lives, families, and relationships back, and He wants to do it through planting humility in our hearts. In place of an ugly, controlling spirit, God can give us a generous and humble heart—a beautiful spirit.

CHAPTER SIX

RESTING IN THE CURRENT
(SURRENDER)

The man who wishes to offer a pure mind to God
but who is troubled by cares
is like a man who expects to walk quickly even though
his legs are tied together.
JOHN CLIMACUS

-◄O►-

LISA AND I WANTED TO MOVE BACK TO WASHINGTON STATE TO BE close to our children's grandparents, but the situation looked bleak. When we discussed our options with a realtor, his scenario stunned us. "Best case scenario is that you'd have to bring $10,000 to settlement." We'd have to *pay* to sell our home, assuming we could find someone willing to buy it.

"How long would we have to stay here to break even?" Lisa asked with the tone of a patient discussing a very painful procedure.

"To walk away without paying anything? I'd give it six years."

My wife and I had prayed extensively about buying this town-house. In every way, God appeared to bless the move. Seven years later, our home was worth considerably less than what we paid for it.

"Why didn't God stop us?" Lisa wondered out loud. After all, we'd given God plenty of opportunities.

One day, while Lisa was praying, a definite impression formed in her thoughts. It was as if God were asking, had she considered that He wanted us in that neighborhood to reach other people rather than to boost our financial equity?

We had to ask ourselves hard questions: Does our understanding leave room for serving a God who would lead us to make what turned out to be a poor financial decision but what also turned out to be a profitable spiritual one? In other words, does obedience obligate God to bless us, or can obedience call us to sacrifice?

Think about the Cross before you answer.

We need to discard our "primitive" Christianity, the one in which each sin merits a whack, and each act of obedience merits one heavenly blessing. We think obedience should lead to blessing after blessing until ultimately we become healthy, wealthy, and wise.

But it's not that simple. Though Jesus promised many blessings, He also *promised* there would be moments of sacrifice: "For everyone will be seasoned with fire, and every sacrifice will be seasoned with salt."[1] When Jesus says *everyone* will be seasoned with fire, He's excluding any exceptions with a startling finality. He's saying there will come a time when you will be asked to sacrifice for the faith.

Are you ready?

It's possible that a Christian political candidate might do everything right — maybe her life is a sterling example of tenacity, perseverance, and godliness — but still lose an election by an embarrassing margin. A Christian businessman might operate his business on the principles of honesty and integrity and still watch bankruptcy enfold him.

Sometimes we need to be reminded that our faith is based on the concept of sacrifice, beginning with Jesus. No one ever lived a more obedient life than Jesus, yet few have ever died such an inhumane death. Israel was enslaved for four hundred years — but never forsaken. The early Christian church was hunted, persecuted, and brutally beaten at various moments in its first century — but always held with great affection by her God.

At other moments in history, the church and her servants have been blessed by opulent abundance. During some of these periods, the most respected position in the community was that held by the local Christian minister. The richest members of the town were often stalwarts in the church.

We don't choose the time or place in which we are born. Surrender to God's purposes is the interior attitude adjustment by which we can live above our time with an eternal perspective. People who live on the surface of life are ruled by circumstances, but surrender lifts us above momentary streams of events. As Paul said, "I have learned the secret of being content in any and every situation, whether well fed or hungry, whether living in plenty or in want."[2]

Faith and surrender are based on the notion that God's good purpose will be worked out whether I see earthly blessing or not[3] and that in the meantime I can experience an interior peace that passes all understanding[4] by adopting a childlike trust. The measure of true faith is not how easy (or difficult) life becomes; it's how we maintain a spirit of surrender through the ups and downs of everyday living.

SO MANY CHILDREN

One of the great difficulties of surrender is that God doesn't appear to treat His children equally.

As we tried to sell our house, a woman in Lisa's Bible study told how God "miraculously" provided a buyer for her house. As the group rejoiced with her, Lisa fought like a guerrilla warrior against the sin of envy.

"Are we ever going to get out?" Lisa asked me, following a long stretch in which not a single prospect walked over my wife's meticulously cleaned floors (with three small children, maintaining such "showable" floors is no mean feat). The unspoken question was, *If God provided for them, why not for us?*

This question is as old as Christianity. After Jesus' resurrection, He had a heart-to-heart talk with Peter, and warned Peter about the kind of death he would face. Peter looked behind him and saw John, so he asked, "Lord, what about him?"

Even though Peter had just been forgiven for denying Jesus three times, he still resented the fact that he might have to die a violent death while John got off more easily.

Jesus refused to answer Peter's question: "If I want him to remain alive until I return, what is that to you?"[5]

In this, Jesus tells you and me that we must surrender our jealousy and envy about God's plan for other people when those plans seem preferable to ours. It is when I compare my situation to that of others that I surrender the precious peace that God wants to give me.

Instead of challenging God's actions on behalf of another, on the matter of our townhouse we had to ask ourselves a more important question: Were we willing to adopt surrender and stay, if that's what

God wanted? At a bare minimum, we needed to accept our circum-stances until God made a way for us to move.

There was great freedom in this for me, and transformation. When I insist on control, my anxiety level rises; frustration reaches a boiling point, and my wife and children are most likely to become my victims. At the moment we needed to be drawing closer, supporting and encouraging one another, we could have become alienated with accusation and unfocused anger. Practicing the virtue of surrender was our key to a stronger family life in the midst of disappointment. If God was changing our plans, we needed to get on board with what *He* was doing rather than become obsessed with what *we* wanted.

Through this process I realized how trials shape us.

NO NEUTRAL TRIALS

Some time ago, I was stunned by looking at high school photographs. I was only ten years out of school at the time and had barely begun to grasp the seasons of life. It never occurred to me that my athletic-look-ing crowd of friends would one day resemble my parents' Bible study. These pictures were my first clue. I couldn't believe how "low" my forehead had been back when I was eighteen. It was just ten years, no more than that, but how I had changed!

Like time, trials will cause us to change. They can leave us with an ugly, bitter, cynical, and mean spirit, or we can use them to become stronger. But we can no more walk through trials unchanged than we can live through a decade unmarked.

How we profit from or are crushed by our trials largely depends upon our state of surrender to God. Many of us came to Christ for very selfish reasons. The second chapter of Matthew tells us that the Magi came to Jesus to worship Him and to bring Him gifts.[6] Even better, Paul came to Jesus to become His servant[7] and he maintained that atti-tude throughout his life.[8] No manner of hardship was able to get Paul off track.

Why have you come to Jesus? To be saved from your sins? So that God would help your financial situation, save your marriage, or pro-vide your children with a "blessed" life?

The virtue of surrender reminds us that we come to Jesus to learn how to be like Him and to offer ourselves as God's servants. If we come to God to be amply provided for, yet find ourselves poor, we'll leave God. If we come to God to be made well, yet find ourselves sick, we'll leave Him. If we come simply to serve Him, no event in life can steal our motivation, for God will always be worthy of our allegiance. If I came to Jesus to acknowledge His place as Lord and every possible door in life slams in my face, my ultimate purpose in life will still be the same—that is, to serve Him.

Christianity without surrender says, "If God blesses me, I'll be obedient. If times get rough, I'll try something else." Christianity born out of surrender is typified by C. S. Lewis's remark, "I was not born to be free. I was born to adore and to obey."[9]

While contemplating this truth of surrender, Jeanne Guyon wrote what may be one of the most profound reflections ever in all of Christian literature outside the Bible: "If you gave yourself to Him to be blessed and to be loved, you cannot suddenly turn around and take back your life at another season when you are being crucified! . . . God gives us the cross, and then the cross gives us God."[10]

Guyon has learned what Paul knew: the wisdom of being thankful for the very thing that most people flee. To experience a hard circumstance that goes against our will, she says, is a gift. When accepted with the right spirit, it becomes an important means to a higher end: the presence of God Himself. As Paul taught, we are coheirs with Christ "*if indeed we share in his sufferings* in order that we may also share in his glory."[11]

When petty grievances threaten to shrink my life into self-pity, the inner discipline of embracing whatever God's will is for me this day leads me into a deepening experience of fellowship with Jesus.

Here's the key for me: Paul reminds me that I'm *sharing* in Christ's sufferings. I'm not suffering alone. I'm not in wealth, ease, sickness, or comfort alone. I'm living life with Christ. My heart's desire is to stay where Christ is. If Jesus leads me through trial or triumph, the most important thing is that I'm with Him. Instead of asking, "Where is relief?" "Where is comfort?" "Where is the easy way out?" I'm led to ask, "Where is God? And what does He want of me in this situation?"

If, like me, you've found yourself chafing under the strain of obedience and service, reflect on this insight: *God gives us the cross, and then the cross gives us God.*

THE PROCESS OF SURRENDER

The key to surrender is acceptance. As Jeanne Guyon wrote, "As soon as anything comes to you in the form of suffering, at that very moment a natural resistance will well up somewhere inside you. When that moment comes, immediately resign yourself to God. Accept the matter."[12] At times, this acceptance will come only after bitter struggle. Be encouraged that your experience will not be substantially different from anyone else's: "Sometimes you may bear the cross in weakness; at other times you may bear the cross in strength. But whether you bear it in weakness or in strength, bear it!"[13]

Sometimes I surrender to God's apparent will quietly, sometimes with great anger and only after a heated discussion with Him. How we come to the point of acceptance may differ; *whether* we come to acceptance should not.

So far, we have been talking about surrender to God in trials, but we can practice surrender in the face of blessings, too.

Shortly after receiving an award for excellence in teaching, Bob Patton was promoted and became a full, tenured professor of finance at a state university. As a result of good money management, self-restraint, and diligent effort, he experienced a relative degree of financial security, which allowed him to begin building a comfortable home on a beautiful lot in Washington state.

As Bob completed this house, painting the final trim, he sensed God saying, "This will never be your house."

Oh great, Bob thought, after all this I'm not going to get to live here.

Bob and his wife Betsy did move in, yet in the past two decades, they've rarely lived alone. Why? Because they took the attitude that the house was *lent* to them. Accordingly, the Pattons have given free room and board to people who have needed it. They've welcomed college and seminary students, families facing financial difficulties, people with physical disabilities, and people in emotional distress who need care for a while.

"The money is mine to manage," Bob explains, "not mine to spend."

Almost two decades ago now, Bob walked away from that secure, set-for-life professorship to become an associate pastor at a then-small church (of which I'm now a member). His spirit of surrender in the midst of earthly blessings has inspired many Christians, including me, to re-examine our assumptions about the management of money and possessions.

Bob and Betsy understand that surrender in the face of earthly blessings means we relinquish that inner sense of "I *deserve* this good stuff! I worked for it, and it's mine." Surrender, for some of us, means keeping our eyes trained on God when we have enough money to last ten lifetimes. For others of us, it's keeping our eyes trained on God even though we're down to oatmeal and raisins five days in a row.

Surrender means adopting the right inner attitude to every outer circumstance: "Whether it be weakness or strength, sweetness or bitterness, temptation, distraction, pain, weariness, uncertainty or blessing, all should be received as equal from the Lord's hand."[14]

If all this sounds difficult, take heart; every thoughtful Christian has struggled with this. In closing, let's look at how we can practice this crucial virtue.

THE POINT OF OUR SURRENDER

Surrender has Christlikeness as its definite goal. "What is the result of walking continually before God in a state of abandonment? The ultimate result is godliness."[15] This only makes sense, doesn't it? If we surrender to God's shaping, it only stands to reason that we'll become more like Jesus.

None of my children are in diapers now, but I remember the difference between putting a diaper on my son and one on my youngest daughter, Kelsey. With Graham, diapering was guerrilla warfare. He had one goal — to get off the table as soon as possible. If naked, so much the better. He rocked and rolled and kicked. I always got the diaper on him in the end, though sometimes he looked like he was wearing it sideways. Kelsey practically thanked us for taking off her wet diapers. She lifted her back so we could scoop the clean diapers under her, and she chatted and smiled as we cleaned. Consequently, she wore a diaper with a perfectly shaped "V" in front and a tightly fitting back.

We can try to resist God, but our character will reveal it. Surrender is not something we can achieve all at once. Don't discount the small battles, thinking you can win the war in one tremendous act of "giving it all up to God." John Climacus warns, "To be unfaithful in the small things is to be unfaithful in the great, and this is very hard to bring under control."[16]

Any small act of surrender, spiritually speaking, may do more good for you than a year's worth of external discipline. "A man who fasts—leaving off all those things his appetite improperly craves—does a good thing. But the Christian *who is fasting from his own desires and his own will, and who feeds upon God's will alone*, does far better."[17] Skipping a meal is nothing compared to relinquishing control. Earnestly pray about offering up a "small surrender."

Above all, we must remember that God's agenda and love for us holds a much bigger concern than supplying our immediate comforts. God's ultimate aim is that we be conformed to the image of Christ[18]—and it is only through that grid that God's goodness can be fully understood. Our understanding of Christ's nature is broken and bent; our true understanding of ourselves is hampered by sin, pride, and self-deception. Only God really knows what needs to be "rubbed off" or "polished up."

To really surrender, then, we need to learn to stop measuring our trials against our comforts, and instead measure our trials against their potential to draw us nearer to God and to make us more like Christ.

As God would have it, our home in northern Virginia eventually sold, and we were able to move back to Washington state. We found a home to rent in Bellingham, and when the weather is right, we can see the tip of Mount Baker from our bedroom window. Of course, we're enormously thankful for this blessing, but I've learned my lesson. Soon after we arrived here, someone asked me, "So, how long do you plan to be in Bellingham?"

"I wouldn't mind retiring here," I admitted. "But that's up to God."

CHAPTER SEVEN

FREEDOM FROM WITHIN
(DETACHMENT)

*If you desire to undertake a devout life, you must not only
cease to sin, but also cleanse your heart from all affections to
sin. . . . Souls that are recovered from the state of sin, and still retain
these affections . . .eat without relish, sleep without rest, laugh
without joy, and drag themselves along rather than walk.
They do good, but with such a spiritual heaviness that it takes
away all the grace from their good exercises.*[1]

FRANCIS DE SALES

◄◯►

F OR ME, THE SADDEST FLOWERS IN ALL THE WORLD WILL ALWAYS BE
yellow roses.

The last time I purchased them was twenty years ago, after the
fifth or sixth breakup with "Sharon." Yellow roses were her favorite.

Sharon and I were involved in a tempestuous relationship during
high school, and, try as we might, we could never quite declare it at an
end. I was much too immature to maintain a long-term relationship, but
I was also too immature to detach myself emotionally from Sharon.

I felt so guilty that every time we decided to end the dates, I went
out of my way to express to Sharon how special I thought she was—
beginning with the yellow roses. And, of course, as these things happen in high school, that was inevitably followed by Sharon being
reminded what a great guy *I* was. And since I thought she was so special and she thought I was so great, maybe we ought to give it "just
one more try. . . ."

It is one thing to be surrendered. It is another thing entirely to
be *detached*. Surrender is an act of the will, accepting physical

circumstances or situations God has ordained and looking for His good purpose in them. Detachment means we stop finding our meaning and security in people, things, positions, money, and power so they no longer lure us into actions we know are unwise or unprofitable.

The most famous verse on detachment is probably Matthew 6:33: "But seek first his kingdom and his righteousness, and all these things will be given to you as well." Jesus is saying that the *focus* and *passionate attachments* of the believer will seem radically at odds with those of the world. Detachment is the attitude that helps us cooperate with God's work as He shapes our desires, so we come to rest in the knowledge that what is truly valuable to the soul can only be given by God Himself: "Delight yourself in the LORD and he will give you the desires of your heart."[2]

FREEDOM FROM WITHIN

Every day, out-of-order and out-of-control appetites hold us in their grip, some to a lesser extent, some greater. John of the Cross teaches that uncontrolled appetites wound us in two ways: They deprive us of experiencing and enjoying God's Spirit, and they "weary, torment, darken, defile and weaken" us.[3]

An undisciplined inner life — one that is attached to the world even as it seeks to fight it — is misery defined. Some of us live spiritually like a person on a diet who has a freezer full of Häagen-Dazs ice cream. If you're serious about the diet, you'll get the ice cream out of the house, right? Otherwise, you'll simply make yourself miserable. We halfheartedly want to follow God and live holy lives, all the while surrounding ourselves with temptation.

We need to understand the mechanics of spiritual temptation. Sometimes, errant desires can become so strong that the desire itself becomes the issue. Even more than the object, the *desire* becomes the idol and motivating force. Once we finally do give in, we're surprised that the fulfillment wasn't nearly as sweet as the anticipation. Once again, the *desire* for the object, more than the object itself, is what tripped us up and caused us to sin — to misuse a person or a thing for our own aggrandizement or to fill some inner void which, ironically, never can be filled.

For several years, I worked in a ministry that reached out to pregnant women. Time and again, we heard the same thing: a young woman didn't really want to begin premarital sex, but she did want intimacy. So she traded her body and never got what she wanted in return. All too often, she felt cheapened and used. Her desire for sex, or for the secure relationship she *thought* it would give her, was a long way from what the sex experience actually delivered.

If you've been caught in the illusions produced by those taunting, tantalizing soul poisons, then you need to experience the freedom and new strength God releases in you when you begin to practice the virtue of detachment.

Let's be practical and honest: It is extremely difficult for us to deny ourselves what we truly desire. The great Reformed writer, John Owen, points out, "He hates not the fruit, who delights in the root."[4] We might have sporadic success at staying away from something that has captivated our heart, but it is unlikely we will have consistent success.

To stop feeding on harmful things, we need to consider our improper appetites: "When the appetites are extinguished — or mortified — one no longer feeds on the pleasure of these things."[5]

Modern evangelicalism can become so focused on stopping a sinful behavior that we can lose the practical nature of virtue. We want to stop sinning without examining and freeing ourselves from the root desires that are disordered. To be free from sin, we need to look at the internal cause rather than just focus on the action. When a Christian falls today, 99 percent of the spiritual effort is spent trying to control the "stumbling" — that is, we focus on outer strategies to help us avoid the situations in which we sin. A young dating couple will be told never to be alone together; an alcoholic will be warned away from bars or liquor stores. But if the heart is bent by an appetite that leads to sin, all the external discipline agreed upon in moments of strength will wilt in the heat of desire.

Iron will — external discipline that creates physical distance but not spiritual deliverance — will meet with only limited success. John of the Cross explains, "We are not discussing the mere lack of things; this lack will not divest the soul if it craves for all these objects. We are dealing with the denudation [we'll explain this word in a moment] of the soul's appetites and gratifications. This is what leaves it free and empty of all things, even though it possesses them. Since the things of the world cannot enter the soul, they are not in themselves an encumbrance . . . rather, it is the will and appetite dwelling within that cause the damage when set on these things."[6]

By *denudation,* John means a nakedness of spirit. God "strips us" of errant longings that lead us into corruption. For our part, we refuse to clothe ourselves with appetites or longings for these things. How? By allowing God to show us how the things we crave never can fill, or cover, the emptiness within, until we long to be clothed in His presence, His will, His purpose, and His character.

If you have been fighting sin unsuccessfully, in large part because while you offer up the action, you can't stop the craving, then you need the virtue of detachment. This virtue begins when we turn our eyes from the created to the Creator.

CHAINS OF SILK

In Victorian novels, romantic tensions often occur when a member of the upper class falls in love with a member of the lower class. Back then, to love someone beneath you in society was considered poor taste. Rather than elevating the person in the lower class, it tended to deflate the reputation of the person from the upper class.

John of the Cross argues that when we love the created over the Creator, we do the same thing: we lower ourselves to the level of what we love. Just as we are raised when we are enraptured by God, so we devalue ourselves when we desire lesser things. "Anyone who loves a creature, then, is as low as that creature and in some ways even lower because love not only equates but even subjects the lover to the loved creature."[7]

When we love something God has created more than we love God Himself, we not only set ourselves up for huge disappointment, but we also set ourselves up to sin against God, over and over. This is the tragedy of our sin: "Since nothing equals God, those who love and are attached to something other than God, or together with Him, offend Him exceedingly."[8]

God offers us spiritual fulfillment, true character transformation, joy, peace — all the intangible blessings that mean the most. But we become fixated by anything else — *everything* else! Instead of interior peace, meaning, freedom, and fulfillment, we crave things that excite the mind, ego, and flesh for a brief moment. And God, who can satisfy every true need, is standing beside us, waiting for us to receive His in-filling, while we set our desire on baser things.

Imagine the satisfaction of a life in which all your holy needs are met by a loving, gracious, generous, and merciful God. There is no danger of manipulation here.

I know a young man who was addicted to heroin. The reason the HIV virus spreads so rapidly among drug abusers is that they often share needles to shoot up immediately after buying a drug. Why? Because they want to make sure the drugs they are buying are genuine, and the only way to do that is to try them out.

The mere thought of buying something to inject into my body when I can't trust the person who is selling it to me is terrifying — but that's the nature of the drug business. It's a manipulative and fearful enterprise.

Not so with God. There is no danger of manipulation, no chance that He won't give us the real thing. If our desire is for Him, we won't be disappointed. Our needs will be met — maybe not in the way that we anticipated, but in the way that is best for the long-term health of our souls.

Imagine the change that might take place in your relationships with others if your deepest needs were being met by a benevolent, ever-present God. You would no longer need to make wearying demands on a spouse. You could become a lover, instead of demanding one. If you were frustrated in your relationship with your parents, you could stop asking for something they couldn't really give, and instead find acceptance and true love from your heavenly Father. If you were a parent, instead of burdening your children with your own expectations, hopes, and ego needs, you could concentrate on equipping them to become who God made them to be.

Demands ruin relationships. Unfulfilled demands turn relationships into a living hell and make us miserable. Unfortunately, it never occurs to most of us to learn how to have God fulfill our needs.

Detachment means that you relinquish every demand you place on things and other created beings — *even legitimate ones.* Demands are nothing more than spiritual chains. François Fénelon warns, "Golden chains are no less chains than are chains of iron."[9] It doesn't matter *what* binds you as long as it binds you. Whether the cords you are entangled with are made of silk or nylon; whether your yoke is made of steel or a beautiful piece of oak; whether your cage is rusted or polished, imprisonment is hell, and your demands are the bars that hold you.

"The road and ascent to God, then, necessarily demands a habitual effort to renounce and mortify the appetites; the sooner this mortification is achieved, the sooner the soul reaches the top. But until the appetites are eliminated, one will not arrive no matter how much virtue one practices."[10]

THE POWER OF DETACHMENT

How can we experience the virtue of detachment? It is an impossible task to slowly disengage ourselves from every errant passion. What we need instead is a powerful war of engagement, which we find by *attaching* ourselves to something else.

When I proposed to my wife, out of love for her I was rejecting every other woman. My affection for Lisa was such that it eclipsed any other romantic interest. *Intense love for something inevitably leads to rejection of something else.* "A more intense enkindling of another, better love (love of one's heavenly bridegroom) is necessary for the vanquishing of the appetites. . . . By finding satisfaction and strength in this love, one will have the courage and constancy to deny readily all other appetites."[11]

One of the surest (but not, admittedly, one of the most mature or most advisable) ways for me to have broken my emotional attachment with Sharon in high school would have been to "fall in love" with someone else. It's easier to leave something if you believe you've found something better. As humans, we don't exist very well in vacuums; we're sucked one way or the other by our passions, so—spiritually speaking—instead of seeking a passion*less* existence, we need to *more intensely focus* our affections. John of the Cross points out that the lure of the world can be so strong that "if the spiritual part of the soul is not fired with other more urgent longings for spiritual things,"[12] the soul won't be able (or it will simply lack the courage) to deny its appetites for the wrong things.

I travel a lot, and there are plenty of temptations on the road. I've heard of many well-known Christian men who refuse to travel alone for this very reason. If somebody books them for a speaking engagement, they require two airline tickets. But what about the salesman from IBM whose boss won't allow such an expense? I wrote an article for a magazine on this very topic, and one of the things I found when talking to others was the fear that some men have before they leave. The entire trip can be reduced to "will I or won't I fall?"

This is an example of a defensive war. God wants more than for us to "not fall" during a business trip. He desires that we be productive, enjoy our time, grow in Him, and perhaps develop some new relationships. If we're obsessed with "not falling," these won't happen.

Instead of fighting a defensive war, go on the offensive. You may want to try to replace your particular obsession with a healthy passion. I suggest this because we don't learn detachment all at once.

One of the things I've done is develop a passion in which I can include God. It's not a religious exercise by any means, but it's a relaxing activity. When I first became interested in becoming a book scout, I viewed all the places I traveled to as locales that might contain that elusive, neglected, and underpriced first edition book. A book scout goes to used bookstores, antique stores, estate sales, and the like, trying to find (in my case) certain modern first editions that are recognized as collectibles.

By the time I give my presentation, exercise, and comb the city for any and all underpriced books, I barely have enough time to catch the plane back home. I can "detach" myself from temptation on the road by "attaching" myself to an enjoyable pursuit. I can create pleasurable memories of character-rich used bookstores rather than litter my life with sinkholes of regret.

This "offensive" principle works just as well at home. Instead of giving in to greed, give something away and experience the pleasure of generosity. Instead of reveling in lust, take time out of your busy schedule to appreciate true beauty. Instead of falling into another addiction, get together with someone and begin discussing how you can make positive changes in your life so that the need for escape becomes less acute.

By repenting of and relinquishing the old desire, we can train ourselves to feed off the new, more noble desire. The enjoyment of our "replacement" may not be immediate, but keep in mind that affection is built over time. If you have fed off an illicit practice for a while, it will take some time to learn to live without it; you can't expect the desire to immediately die. This is where discipline can be marginally helpful, for habits become less forceful the longer we stay away from them.

We need to cover all these activities with a proper romance toward God. Many Christians struggle with their desire for God largely because they've never been taught *how* to love Him; or when they are taught to relate to Him, they're given a simplistic formula (such as a quiet time — twenty minutes of prayer, twenty minutes of worship, twenty minutes of Bible study, every morning). While this discipline can be helpful, it's rarely sufficient to meet our deep-seated longings. We need to expand our understanding of prayer.

Most of the people reading this book are likely to have spent time reading the Bible, expanding their mental understanding of God. You've also probably listened to sermons, maybe even gotten a degree in theology. But have you learned how to increase your *adoration* of God? What have you done to build your heart's passion toward the Almighty?[13]

The idea is to build a complete life with constructive recreation and meaningful work and relationships so the yearnings that so often lead to sin have less of a place in our lives. This is part of the ancient practice of mortification — removing the cause of sin even before temptation strikes. The ancients recognized that while it is possible to deny strong desires, it is more productive to empty these desires before they present themselves.

THE GOOD TRADE

In sixteenth-century Spain, a man named Nicolas became exceedingly wealthy, and in those days, that meant exceedingly powerful as well. Nicolas loved and sought money, and he made more of it in banking and financial transactions than other men made in peddling goods and services.

Nicolas's skill became so pronounced that an archbishop asked him to patch the shaky hull of the archbishopric's financial ship. Nicolas had it floating so well and so quickly that even the king took notice and invited Nicolas into his court. The king reasoned that what Nicolas could do for God, he could also do for God's servant, His Royal Highness.

Nicolas increased the king's holdings to such an extent that he became a daily presence at court. By the age of thirty-seven, Nicolas had reached the highest strata of society. He could afford anything he wanted, and his words were taken seriously by the highest powers in the land. Then he met a tiny, penniless, balding, and seemingly powerless man, whose teachings we have already encountered—John of the Cross.

In league with a nun named Teresa of Avila, John had started a new order of Carmelites, known for their austerity, poverty, and simple rule of life. While Nicolas had everything after which most people aspire, John lived the common man's worst nightmare—he wore no shoes, he traveled cross-country with minimal clothing and often without food, and he was pledged to sexual abstinence.

Yet after meeting John, Nicolas left the court, gave away his money, and entered the Discalced (shoeless) Carmelite order. The man who once walked on palace floors now *by choice* walked barefoot on the stony, sometimes snowy, roads of Spain.

Nicolas responded to the same call that led fishermen to drop their nets and follow Jesus. It was the same inner detachment that centuries later would lead my friend Bob Patton to change his career when he was just reaching his prime as a professor.

Throughout the centuries, Christians have found great meaning, purpose, and fulfillment in spurning the very things that so many people crave. But it would be a gross distortion to define Nicolas's new life by what he left behind. The truth is, he embraced something even better, and that's the real key to detachment. By opening his heart to adopt the spirit and attitudes of Jesus Christ, he began removing himself from the lusts of the flesh. His heart was touched by prayer in a way it was never touched by gold, power, or influence.

Detachment is about far more than merely abstaining from sin. Its practice begins with the delight of our soul, Jesus Christ. When we look at the model of Christian living—Christ Himself—we can immediately see how central detachment was to His existence.

Jesus detached Himself from heaven to become man. He detached Himself from His parents to take up the public ministry of the Messiah. He detached Himself from His people's favor to become their Savior. He detached Himself from life on earth to die for our sins. He detached Himself from spiritually experiencing His Father's presence so He could become sin for us.

Everything that matters most, Christ gave up. And *He is the model for how we live the faith.* Do you want to experience Jesus in a new way? Look for Him in the virtue of detachment.

God calls us to learn detachment, and it is no shame to admit we are still in kindergarten where this is concerned. Most of us struggle with petty sins, jealousies, and attitudes that make us miserable. This is where I suggest we begin: by allowing God to search our hearts and show us truthfully what it is we are craving.

The detached Christian is the one who experiences inner freedom. Shorn of ambition, greed, jealousy, avarice, gluttony, lust, or manipulation, the detached Christian is able to enjoy a new dimension of happiness very few ever find in this world. Ironically, spiritual detachment is the only way to truly enjoy the *physical* world, which God made for our pleasure. Without the gap we build by detachment between us and created things, our desire for the objects and pleasures of this world will overstep its bounds. Our enjoyment always will be reduced to unsatisfied craving.

There is so much strength to be found in detachment. We learn to let go, not just of the action of sin, but of the desire that drives us. Fall in love with God and let Him shape your desires. Refuse to feed off errant passions, and allow God to give you your life back from the cravings and pinings that have distressed you thus far.

But how? you ask. How do I "delight myself in the Lord"? As you may be comprehending at this point, the virtues of Christ do not stand alone; they build on each other. To truly experience the freedom of detachment, we must grow in the spiritual virtue of attachment—the virtue of love—which we'll discuss in the next chapter.

CHAPTER EIGHT

THE ENERGY OF YOUR SOUL
(LOVE)

The soul needs no other force to draw it
than the weight of love.

JEANNE GUYON

YOU ONLY WIN WARS BY GOING ON THE OFFENSIVE. WINSTON Churchill knew the principle, and it tortured him. He found himself at a terrible moment in history, with mainland Europe occupied by the Nazis, and this old principle of war put him to the test.

In this case, going on the offensive meant storming the beaches of French Normandy, though doing so would be a logistical nightmare unparalleled in the history of warfare. As historian Stephen Ambrose explains it, getting the troops ready for D-Day would be like moving Green Bay, Racine, and Kenosha—"every man, woman, and child, every automobile and truck—to the east side of Lake Michigan, in one night."[1]

Not only must all the personnel and material arrive at the right time, but the weather must hold out, the beaches must support the tanks and armored carriers, and the Allies' desperate attempts at surprise must be successful. If Hitler guessed right about the Allies' landing, he could make the going far too ugly for Allied troops to be successful.

This is what tortured Churchill and the other Allied commanders. There were a thousand or more ways this campaign could fail; a thousand reasons why they should not even attempt it. But there was one reason to try that overshadowed everything else: If they succeeded, they were well on the way to winning the war.

Adolf Hitler was also well aware of a principle, one that he chose to ignore. His mentor, Frederick the Great, had warned that "He who defends everything, defends nothing." Hitler believed that his empire demanded absolute defense of every inch of ground he had gained. That belief may have cost him his empire as his forces were spread too thin.

We can learn much from these two examples. Jesus taught that "every tree that does not produce good fruit will be cut down and thrown into the fire."[2] In this, Jesus teaches us to be "offensive" in our faith. Too often, we're obsessed with not producing bad fruit and avoiding mistakes, but the history of God's people is a history in which apathy, inaction, and unfruitfulness anger God more than anything else. It's the perpetually dormant trees that get cut down.

When we try to defend everything, we defend nothing. We need to be offensive-minded, busy concentrating on bearing good fruit.

That's why we need an affinity with God, a movement of the soul that keeps nudging our hearts in His direction. When it comes to Christian spirituality, idling in neutral is a danger. We need something that will overcome the luxurious allure of the world and the many false gods which compete for our affections. What we need is the virtue known as *love*.

What does it mean to love God? I like a phrase from Guyon's work: "To give your whole heart to God is to have all the energy of your soul always centered on Him."[3]

Think about that. Love is merely *focusing the energy of your soul on God*. There's a wonderful example of this in the book of Luke.

A "sinful" woman, likely a prostitute, walked in on one of Jesus' visits with the Pharisees.[4] Seeing Jesus, she fell before Him and astonished everyone by pouring out most of her life savings, spent on a costly fragrant oil, over His feet. Obviously, she was not thinking about her financial future. She was enraptured, and the energy of her soul was centered on the Messiah. He had touched her spirit in a way no one else ever could, and she responded with beautiful and reckless adoration.

That's love.

Becoming like Christ is a life's work. It requires the only energy in the universe that is inexhaustible: love, and in particular, the love of God. No less an intellectual than Jonathan Edwards warns, "Man's nature is very lazy, unless he is influenced by some affection such as love, hate, desire, hope or fear. These emotions are like springs that set us moving in all the affairs of life and its pursuit."[5]

Without the engine of love, we will be lackadaisical about our faith and everything that matters.

ENEMIES OF LOVE

Before the Allies dared approach Normandy, they spent months evaluating the enemy's position, strength, force, and will. They wanted to know what they were up against. What enemies do we face as we seek to live out the ideal expressed by Jesus when He urged us to "love the Lord your God with all your heart and with all your soul and with all your mind"?[6]

The first enemy is apathy. Dorothy Sayers wrote a generation ago that "sin that believes in nothing, cares for nothing, seeks to know nothing, interferes with nothing, enjoys nothing, hates nothing, finds purpose in nothing, lives for nothing, and remains alive because there is nothing for which it will die."

Have you met people like this? They don't seem to care about *anything*. Because of its self-deceiving subtlety, apathy can be a greater danger to our faith than outright rebellion. Someone in rebellion at least understands the issues — and rejects God. An apathetic person doesn't even care about what's at stake.

Another enemy of love is anger and resentment. A pastor might find his intestines churning when people do not appreciate his hard work or teaching. A mother could quietly seethe over the disability of a child. A married couple could simmer over a battle with infertility. These angers are the spiritual-intimacy blockers of our age. Too often, we have extremely high expectations and bitterly resent the frustration of even one unfulfilled dream. Anger destroys the posture of humility and it chafes against surrender — those load-bearing foundation walls of our faith.

A third enemy of love is fear and a corresponding lack of trust. You can never "rest" in the presence of an abusive or violently explosive person, because you know that an eruption could take place at any given moment. If your view of God is a suspicious one—when is He going to punish me next?—you'll have a difficult time entering into true intimacy.

Think about it this way: Who *wouldn't* resist a tyrannical, uncaring, or aloof being? If my heart perceives God this way, of course I'm not going to want to draw close to Him. Just as it would be difficult to make love to my spouse while wearing a suit of armor, so it becomes difficult to pray when I surround myself with spiritual shields, always putting up a defense against God.

A fourth enemy of love is over-commitment. Many of us never choose to grow cold toward God, we just get caught up in everything else.

There's yet a fifth enemy of love: Our Westernized fear and suspicion of emotions. I'm all for reciting creeds and knowing doctrine. But an intellectually astute mind is never sufficient apart from a passionate heart. What we believe is crucially important, but the energy of our being—our emotions—is also important. Edwards points out that "He who has only doctrinal knowledge and theory, without affection, is never engaged in the goodness of faith."[7]

Of course, we can pay too much attention to feelings and let them sweep us away. Of course, our faith is true whether we are passionate about it or not. But near rejection of emotions comes at a great cost, for without emotions we love too little. Without love, we change too little. And without change—here's the primary point—we will never become holy. For holiness means being separated in heart to God and purely His own, with nothing left of distrust or resistance between us.

This might sound dramatic, but it's true: If you want to become holy, you must first become passionate. "No change of religious nature will ever take place unless the affections are moved."[8]

The apostle Paul demonstrates this beautifully. Because of the intensity of his love, Paul can no longer think of himself apart from the object of his devotion. He even dares to say, "For to me, to live is Christ. . . . "[9] These are the words of a man who has focused the energy of His soul on the God he loves. He reveals a love that Climacus calls an "inebriation of the soul."[10] He's drunk on love.

What's in your heart? What keeps you from loving God? Is it apathy? Anger and resentment? Fear? An over-committed schedule? Discomfort with emotion?

THE HEART OF LOVE

My family went on a walk recently, and my youngest daughter (then five years old), kept talking about how she had to find somebody "just like daddy" to marry. "I'm going to marry *you*," Kelsey said finally, somewhat defiantly.

"I'm already married," I protested.

"Well, Mommy will just have to find somebody else."

It's gratifying when my kids obey me, but it's miraculously fulfilling when they declare their love and devotion. And it's overwhelming to me that I can stir God's heart just as Kelsey stirred mine. In fact, to do so is my place as a faithful son.

The "horror of horrors" in Scripture is a hard heart. In Mark 3:5 we read that Jesus was "grieved" over the Pharisees' "hardness of heart." (NKJV) We are told that, of all things, "Do not harden your hearts."[11]

What *is* a hardened heart? It is a heart that has stopped feeling, a heart that is dead toward God, a heart that feels no passion — and so it evokes no obedience to His commands.

What will help us obey God's commands is an *engaged* heart, a heart that is enlarging in love, a heart that feels new things, and feels them more deeply than it did before. "I will run in the way of Your commandments, for *You shall enlarge my heart*."[12]

Engaging my heart or enlarging my heart to do the best for God and other people doesn't come easily to me. I've grown up with a theological, intellectual bent and, like many Western Christians, I've cultivated a rather "disembodied" faith. I largely worship God in spite of my body rather than incorporating it (beyond occasionally lifting my hands or kneeling in prayer). God has challenged me in this, sometimes even providing experiences that don't quite make sense to me.

There was a time in my life when my heart had grown hard. There were sins — always repented of, certainly, but not always put to death. In fact, I drifted more than just a little while, and the drift carried me for a few years. Finally, I decided to take a major step to end it. I sat down with another Christian and had a "heart to heart." I've often found that confession does wonders for helping me to address my faults more seriously.

The next Sunday I was worshiping at church. At the time we were still living in Virginia, where we attended a charismatic Episcopalian congregation, and as we moved from one point in the liturgy and began singing a chorus, I lifted my hands and felt a kind of burning in my physical being. As the iciness moved out of my soul, a new excitement surged through my body as well.

I had experienced this intensity years before, and it brought me to tears to have God acknowledge my desire to once again be completely, unreservedly His. To me, it was God's way of saying, "I've noticed, I'm pleased, I love you."

Christianity requires a tough fight. A tough, tough fight. It is wrong, because it is a sidetrack, to *seek* emotionalism in worship, or to *seek* physical phenomena. But we need every weapon that God will give us, and a heart that is passionately engaged with God and His children is a powerful weapon. Don't fear the full range of human experience.[13]

Do you want to become holy? Then open your heart and learn to feel deeply. Ask God for the virtue of love. Quit shutting off your emotions; in doing so, you're needlessly limiting your chance to grow.

THE RELATIONAL SIDE OF HOLINESS

The musical play *Grease* portrays the transformation of a "pure, innocent" young woman who joins a leather-wearing, cigarette-smoking crowd at her high school. Her decision isn't based on the thought that leather is more comfortable than cotton or that cigarettes might be good for her. It's based solely on her relationship with a young man.

A physically passionate relationship is a powerful experience. It can shape us for good or for ill. A spiritually passionate relationship has the same impact.

We celebrate Paul's glorification of love in 1 Corinthians 13, but the man who wrote, "the greatest of these is love" was just a few decades removed from passionately persecuting and murdering Christ's followers. As a young man, Paul had to scrape dried blood from beneath his fingernails, figuratively if not literally. Paul was intense. We do damage to this passage if we give it a sentimental rendering, or imagine Paul as a soft, somewhat effeminate man. Love is the force that powered the transformation of Paul's life.

Never underestimate the power of love to change a human heart. Such a radical reorientation results not from a change of mind, but from a change of passion and allegiance. In fact, our holiness never begins with rule keeping, but with a passionate relationship. If we love someone, we're reluctant to offend them.

John Climacus urges us, "We should love the Lord as we do our friends. Many a time I have seen people bring grief to God, without being bothered about it, and I have seen these very same people resort to every device, plan, pressure, plea from themselves and their friends, and every gift, simply to restore an old relationship upset by some minor grievance."[14]

If we cultivate an attachment for God, our desire and thirst for temporal sins, bad habits, and sinful attitudes will slowly fade. "The fresh taste of spiritual things keeps Christians from worldly contentments."[15]

Where many Christians go wrong is trying to detach without first attaching. Of course it's possible to have nothing more than warm feelings toward God and live a virtuous life, but why would you want this? Besides which, a life of virtue and obedience without passion requires a level of discipline most of us will never attain.

How do we build a passionate relationship with God?

1. Ask God to help you

Scripture can be so incredibly practical. James writes, "If any of you lacks wisdom, he should ask God, who gives generously to all without finding fault, and it will be given to him" (1:5). If you have less attachment to God than you need to grow in holiness, stop right now and pray, "Lord, give me a love for You that is more powerful than any hunger for sin."

Do you think God will hear that prayer and say, "Let me consider whether I really want to answer that one"? Not a chance.

2. Order your attachments

My wife thought I was the cruelest husband on earth. We had just purchased a car with a stick shift, and I was trying to teach her how to drive it. After practicing on flat ground, I took her to a side street with a steep hill.

Lisa looked at me like I was crazy, then let out the brake. The car started to roll backward. She slammed on the brakes, sending both of us flying toward the windshield.

"I can't do this," she said. "I'll wreck your new car."

"You'll get it right," I promised.

Lisa scowled.

Fortunately, both our car and our marriage survived the ordeal.

Maybe you can remember the first time you drove a stick shift. There's a delicate balancing maneuver that you have to learn — not too much gas, not too much clutch. You have to learn to let one out in precise proportion to pushing the other in.

The same "balancing maneuver" is necessary in Christian growth. We become attached and detached by degrees, and we need to be thoughtful to know how the two are playing against each other at any given time.

There are some times when I may watch television several nights a week, but there will be other times when the Spirit warns me to take some time off. There will be seasons when I am perhaps overly active in ministry and seasons when God calls me to rest.

There are times when I have to say to myself regarding changes that don't come quickly, "Take it easy, Gary. You'll get there. Be patient with yourself and just give it time." And there are other occasions when I say, "You've put up with this long enough. It's time to press on."

One of the things that can drive evangelical Christians crazy is that love points beyond hard and fast "rules." When dealing with matters of the heart, something that is not inherently sinful can still get in the way. On the other hand, sometimes love tells us to rest and "lighten up." Ordering your attachments is an art more than a science. It involves vigilance and discernment, two virtues of Christ we will discuss in upcoming chapters.

3. Avoid competing attachments

It takes me about ninety seconds to eat a bag of M & M's. It takes me about thirty minutes on an exercise bike to work off the calories. (Would that it were the other way around!) In the same way, spiritual leeches — sins, bad habits, bad attitudes — attach themselves to my soul in seconds, but it can take weeks to work them off.

As I go through my day, I can't consciously focus every minute on loving God. But I can keep a careful eye on the things I allow to draw my attention and my affections, the way I can responsibly monitor how much candy I consume. Proverbs 4:23 says, "Above all else, guard your heart, for it is the wellspring of life." It is easy to smother our love for God when we allow it to be covered over by competing affections.

4. Meditate on the loveliness of God

Meditation is a natural practice for a captivated heart. Climacus writes, "Someone truly in love keeps before his mind's eye the face of the beloved and embraces it there tenderly. Even during sleep the longing continues unappeased, and he murmurs to his beloved."[16]

Sometimes I'll "meditate" on my children. Just recently, I watched my youngest, Kelsey, walk toward the car from our front door. I delighted in the cute little coat she was wearing, the way she had her hair pulled back, and the melodramatic caution she used when approaching the concrete steps. I wanted to burn that image into my mind because she felt so precious to me.

With God, there's a direct correlation between seeing Him with the eyes of faith, thinking about Him, and being bound by the cords of love. I may use a Bible verse; I may look at something in creation; I may just lovingly repeat the name, "Jesus," but I look to find ways to train my spiritual eyes on God.

Love has led individuals to abdicate thrones, relinquish inheritances, and move to foreign lands. Attachment to another person is truly a powerful experience. Attachment to God is an experience that changes us forever.

CHAPTER NINE

SAFE RELATIONSHIPS
(CHASTITY)

God is such a stickler about morality, not because he wants to control our behavior, but because he wants us to become the kind of people who can see him and thus experience infinite joy.

PETER KREEFT

IN A SOUTHERN CALIFORNIA WAREHOUSE, VCRS ARE STACKED FROM floor to ceiling, copying videotapes twenty-four hours a day, five days a week. All this effort goes to produce pornographic films for one of the most successful enterprises of our age, Evil Angel Video (the company's real name), founded by pornography mogul John Stagliano.[1]

Porn has become so commercially successful and mainstream that it even has its own industry trade publication, *Adult Video News*. The *News* claims that the number of X-rated video rentals rose from 75 million in 1985 to *665 million* in 1996. In 1996, over *$8 billion* was teased out of consumers' hands to purchase time in the presence of sex and nudity.

Add up all that our country spends on Broadway productions, and regional and nonprofit theaters; throw in total revenues for opera, ballet, jazz, and classical music performances—and you have less than the revenues for strip clubs *alone*.[2] If I could wave a wand and wipe out lust, "we would be plunged into the greatest economic depression in history."[3]

Lust has gone mainstream. *Chastity* is the true alternative lifestyle. Preach perversion and people will die to defend your "rights." Preach chastity and you'd better hire a lawyer.

To be *chaste* means, simply, to be sexually pure. As a heart attitude, it means more than that. Chastity recognizes that, though sexuality is part of everyone's being, we are all also spiritual beings, and because all of us are created by God we must treat others with respect and dignity. If lust leads to using people for our pleasure, then true chastity, as an attitude of heart, leads to protecting people for the sake of their wholeness.

BATTLING THE BEAST

Lust is no more a stranger to the church than it is to our society. A Promise Keepers survey found that 65 percent of the men at their conferences confessed that lust was their biggest struggle. I've heard that a major hotel said its rentals of adult channels reached an all-time high during a youth pastors' convention. As one seminarian confided to me, "I don't think I'd go out and buy a pornographic magazine, but I wouldn't want to be left alone in a locked room with one." While many Christian men would not visit a prostitute or have an affair, they often succumb in the face of fantasy images. After all, they rationalize, it's not the same as real sexual involvement with another person. And it's just the push of a button away on any television or computer screen.

Kreeft insists that sexual sin as an outer act "may be the widest road, but it is not the deepest pit."[4] The "pit" could be likened to the darkness of our heart, from which a predatory attitude toward sex springs.

How can we face down this dark, driving force in our lives?

Long ago, I found some very practical advice in ancient rather than modern writings. John Climacus writes about experiencing chastity through a deep-heart change: "The man who struggles against this enemy by sweat and bodily hardships is like someone who has tied his adversary with a reed." Many Christians have experienced the ineffectiveness of trying to avoid lustful thoughts until, in fact, they are obsessing about sex.

John admitted that developing spiritual disciplines was a somewhat more effective approach. By building discipline, we can enjoy a certain strength against temptation. But there's a stronger antidote: "If he fights [lust] with humility, calmness, and thirst [for righteousness and God], it is as though he had killed the enemy and buried him in sand."[5]

The strongest antidote is internal change, partaking in the divine nature of God. Peter Kreeft is a modern writer who understands this same dynamic. Kreeft says: "Concentrating on gluttony does not usually cure gluttony, especially in its serious stages, for it focuses attention on the very addiction or obsession that we want to escape. The same principle is true for lust. Though it sounds irresponsible and simplistic, we must 'turn our back on our problem' and look to God as our joy, our end, our fulfillment, our all, for the simple reason that he *is*." [6]

THE ROOTS OF LUST

At Lacy Township High School, officials who were concerned about rumors of sexual improprieties on the part of faculty and staff passed a rule ordering all adult personnel to approach the students with "extreme caution." As one writer described it, "No touching, no hugs, no possibly suspicious pats on the shoulder, and when face to face with a student at a distance of less than three feet, the teachers and custodians were to raise both arms above their heads in a gesture of surrender."[7]

See how silly we look when we try to replace a virtue with bureaucracy? Though "sexual freedom" promised to connect us, lust has turned us into ridiculous dupes.

What are the roots of this lust which has so profoundly affected our culture . . . and us as individuals?

Hunger for Intimacy. It's hard to have a ticker-tape parade when you don't have a main street. That problem faced the New Jersey Devils hockey team in 1995 after they won the Stanley Cup. When most of your fan base lives in the Jersey suburbs, what town do you choose for the celebration? The team management held the celebration on an asphalt parking lot outside the Meadowlands.

This small incident signals a major shift in our society — the disconnectedness and relative anonymity of our lives. Public opinion and community disapproval are nonexistent for most of us, as many people don't even know their immediate neighbors. The peer pressure that contained lust and shameful behavior in previous generations has been largely removed in today's cities and larger suburbs. It's when the youth pastors were out of town, behind a locked door, and *anonymous* that they fell.

This disconnectedness can create an endemic spiritual loneliness. When people feel alienated from each other, the desire for intimacy becomes a gnawing ache. The temptation is to take shortcuts, and lust creates an immediate false feeling of intimacy and connectedness.

Why do we accept substitute intimacy? Because meaningful intimacy requires work. You have to learn how to listen, respect, forgive, encourage, support, tolerate, and give — to bury your selfishness, and put someone else before you. You make mistakes and feel ashamed, and you're tempted to kill the relationship and start over. You learn how to persevere.

Lust *looks* like intimacy . . . without all the necessary personal growth and responsibility. You don't have to worry about deep character issues such as forgiveness, humility, and patience. There's no need for a man to have to face his pride, disrespect, and selfishness when he looks at pornography. There's no need for a woman to face issues of pettiness and manipulation with the "dreamboat" man who is starring in her latest cheap romance novel. She'll never have to say, "I'm sorry I put you down in front of your friends."

These paper transactions (or the ones on TV or video) which we use to feed the lustful beast within only cheapen us. They make us unhealthy and evil in our demands and evaluations of the real people in our lives.

The virtue of chastity, however, makes rich and satisfying relationships possible. And healthy relationships shape us into healthy people. If the root of lust is a hunger for intimacy, then we can start to resolve the need by building appropriate, responsible intimacy into our lives.

Idolatry. Why do you think our culture developed the term *sex goddess?* The apostle Paul warns that in our fallen state, we are tempted to worship the created rather than the Creator.[8] While ancient societies worshiped the stars and moon, we worship washboard abdomens, tight derrières, and shapely legs.

Becoming captivated by the things of the flesh is a form of idolatry. It begins when, through an inner spiritual weakness, *appreciation* descends into *obsession.*

Now let's be clear about something: It is possible to notice a woman's (or man's) personal beauty without failing in our marital vows. In fact, appreciation of another's beauty can actually be channeled into thanksgiving offered to God. John Climacus writes of Nonnus, the holy bishop of Heliopolis, who, "having looked on a body of great beauty, at once gave praise to its Creator and after one look was stirred to love God. . . . " Recognizing the deeper truth he was witnessing, Climacus remarked, "It was marvelous how something that could have brought low one person managed to be the cause of a heavenly crown for another."[9]

This is where the gift of chastity comes in, for "to the pure, all things are pure."[10] A spiritually healthy heart allows me to enter into a genuine, soul-satisfying appreciation of beauty. I cheapen my own soul by allowing myself to look upon someone with an obsessive, inappropriate hunger.

Hunger for Heaven. It may sound odd to say that a root of lust is a hunger for heaven. But heaven is bliss, escape from the pressures and responsibilities of this life—and lust is a way of escaping into a cheap imitation of the real bliss our heart longs for. Why wait for heaven's bliss when I can get cheap doses of escape right now?

Dr. Dan Allender writes, "Destructive lust is fueled by a determination to make life more palatable and perfect than it can possibly be in a fallen world."[11]

He continues: "Lustful fantasies are an effort to escape the humdrum daily grind of cleaning up Play-Doh and washing the 1,000[th] diaper. It may also be the means to flee from the terror of making a presentation to the board of elders. Fantasies are private magic carpets that serve to deliver the soul from boredom, anxiety, anger, loneliness, and rage to a 'better' world that offers momentary relief and satisfaction.

"Lust is the effort to . . . be lifted out of our current struggles into a world that feels (for an instant) like the Garden of Eden. . . . [L]ust is our effort to push our way back into the garden."[12]

Armed with this understanding, when I experience the loneliness, the vanity, the "what's-it-all-about" sense of this world I remind myself, "What I *really* want is heaven. What I feel is a hunger for a perfect world that is coming, but which I can't fully experience yet."

Waiting for that world rather than demanding an immediate

release through a lustful experience is, in itself, a meaningful exercise in soul growth. The tension and boredom I want to escape will one day be removed, but in the present, God asks me to direct my energies toward solving problems rather than escaping them.

Hunger for Power and Control. There is something inherently consuming about sex. Sexual fantasies often revolve around conquest or capture.[13] Illicit sex can turn malicious very quickly. "Destructive lust is the intersection of desire and destruction, and emptiness and vengeance."[14] This is where sex can become hurtful and even violent, and at the very least degrading.

It goes without saying that this attitude can hardly coexist with the character of Christ.

The malicious nature of lust reduces a human being to a shallow veneer. Lust is an emotionally violent act, an absurd and degrading reduction of another person's value. Eventually, unguarded lust has led many men and women to destroy their own homes because flesh-and-blood people who are aging can never fulfill fantasies.

This is the demonic heart of lust revealed: It comes in masquerading as love, while devouring the soul with its spirit of malice.

If lust is the shortcut that leads to destruction of intimacy and the destruction of self, how is it that the long, patient road to meaningful relationships leads through *chastity?* How does a balanced self-containment lead to self-giving and deeper human bonds than we've imagined possible? It is to the virtue of chastity and its underlying attitude that we now turn.

THE ROOTS OF CHASTITY

1. A Divine Romance

One of the most shocking conversations of my life was with a former Bible study leader whose battle with lust brought him down and led him to ask Jesus "out" of his life.

The shocking part was his admission of almost attempting rape. Though he stopped short of the act, he seriously contemplated it.

What went wrong in this man's life? There were a number of things, but one of them was that he admitted going through "religious motions" without having the needs of his soul met. He developed a ravenous appetite for pornography, which never ultimately satisfied him. His gnawing spiritual hunger, darkened by the arousal of porn, became so intense that it took a malicious turn, and women became objects of his anger.

Thomas Aquinas points out in his *Summa* that "those who find no joy in spiritual pleasures turn to the pleasures of the body."[15] It is spiritual emptiness that leads us to lust. In contrast, the root of chastity is spiritual fulfillment. Climacus writes, "A chaste man is someone who has driven out bodily love by means of divine love, who has used heavenly fire to quench the fires of the flesh."[16]

We begin to experience the freedom of chastity by cultivating our awareness and thirst for the holy presence of God. Those who preach maintaining sexual purity via excessive activity are trying to "outrun" sexual temptation. But merely running from sin is a spiritually draining and futile exercise. If we don't get to the core of the matter, we'll never be free to encounter God. What we need is a passionate and enriching relationship with God.

2. Create realistic expectations

If you struggle with lust and want God to give you religious feelings that will equal or exceed the rush you get from sin, you may well be disappointed. Your heart may not beat as fast when you walk into church as it did when the man with whom you had an affair first touched your arm. A man who has struggled with pornography may not get the same "rush" from the Bible as he did when he picked up a skin magazine.

Freedom is found when we cultivate a taste for the long-term meaning God gives our lives, as opposed to the short-term excitements of the flesh. This doesn't happen overnight. Rather, like changing your diet over time by the small choices you make, you can cultivate a taste for what will bring the most meaning into your life over the long run.

For example, when the temptation of lust arises, consciously work through the pros and cons. If you've fallen in this area before, you are well aware of the turmoil, stress, and pain it brings. You're familiar with sin's tendency to over-promise and under-deliver. Armed with this knowledge, make a firm decision to forgo the sin "just this once." And try an experiment: Compare the twenty-four hours after making a holy choice with the twenty-four hours after the last time you gave in to lust.

If you remain strong, you'll likely find that this simple act of obedience can create a quiet sense of meaning, fulfillment, and warm satisfaction. This is far more enjoyable than the intense rush of illicit pleasure, which is usually followed by a period of guilt and regret. The peace and dignity you feel when you've redirected your desire is part of God giving your life back. You're trading a few rush-filled moments for a longer, quiet fulfillment. You're creating a history you want to remember, not a moment of weakness you wish you could forget.

Emotionally, I couldn't sustain a euphoric relationship with either my wife or my God. I'd be dead to the world and the other relationships and responsibilities from which I derive so much meaning and satisfaction.

Chastity points us to a higher, deeper, and ultimately quieter existence. It offers a foundational stability to replace the empty personality that is always anxiously looking for the next high. Chastity is not founded on an ecstatic religious high, but on a relationship that silently and confidently carries us to eternity.

3. Cultivate selflessness

Christian men in particular can be notoriously self-centered when it comes to their repentance concerning lust. I've heard men confess their shame, self-loathing, and angst after being caught using pornography, visiting a strip club, or having sex with an unmarried woman. But too frequently they are shockingly insensitive to the plight of the women they've just used.

We need to grow past self-centered repentance, based on the shame of being caught or admitting our sin, to a higher appreciation of how our sin assaults others. To make real spiritual progress is to understand the harm we have done to another person.

Likewise, women involved with married men need to look not only at the pain they've caused themselves but the pain they poured on that man's family. Single Christians need to become acutely aware of the emotional and spiritual scars they cause by having sex with each other.

Lust is a self-centered sin, and it is not overcome by a self-centered repentance.

The solution is to consider others—not merely to be a little thoughtful, but to ask God to give you a respectful reverence for the people He has made. Ask Him to transform your heart, releasing you from the desire to control and use, and to give you a sense of the holiness of His sons and daughters. A life that reverences others has fewer regrets, deeper relationships, and ultimately much more satisfaction.

4. Practice healthy sexual expression

Chastity is too often associated with a prudish attitude that sex is dirty and distasteful. The ancients did not hold this view, not even monks who practiced celibacy.

Aquinas notes that an aversion to sex is a vice, not a virtue.[17] Kreeft adds, "Not only is sexual desire not sinful, it is sometimes a moral obligation."[18] Paul commands those who are married not to unreasonably withhold sexual activity.[19] Song of Songs, a biblical book that is frequently (and understandably) skipped over in Sunday school, celebrates the near intoxication of physical passion.

Sexual enjoyment and celebration is not the same as the misdirected fire of lust.

As a spouse, I have an obligation to my wife to be the outlet for her sexual passion. According to Scripture, the only love life she can righteously have is the love life I'm willing to give to her. And the love I give her must include respect and cherishing.

This is as true for a woman as it is for a man. If either spouse seeks to meet spiritual emptiness by making unreasonable or immoral sexual demands—turning sex into a performance demand—then, frankly, sex becomes abusive.

When Hebrews says to let "the marriage bed [be] kept pure,"[20] we too often limit this to mean physically pure. How many Christians pollute the marriage bed by selfishness, demands, lack of respect, arrogance, or any number of interior vices? We cannot hide behind our wedding rings on this one. Selfishness is selfishness; it is sin.

How does this step apply to the single Christian? The need to preserve and express healthy sexuality is a good reason to seek marriage, among other balancing reasons, of course. Our culture is obsessed with the emotional experience of "falling in love," but the Bible speaks of seeking an outlet for physical desires—so that you can live a holy life—as one of the purposes of marriage.[21] (Not the *only* reason, but a real and legitimate reason.)

The demon Screwtape points out our society's confusion in this regard: "Humans who have not the gift of continence can be deterred from seeking marriage as a solution because they do not find themselves 'in love,' and, thanks to us, the idea of marrying with any other motive seems to them low and cynical. Yes, they think that. They regard the intention of loyalty to a partnership for mutual help, for the preservation of chastity, and for the transmission of life, as something lower than a storm of emotion."[22]

To remain chaste, to create a family, and to assist another throughout life—these are holy and valid reasons to marry. Hollywood has it exactly backwards in this regard, valuing a short-lived emotional attachment over reasoned judgment.

THE BLESSINGS OF CHASTITY

Chastity can help create a beautiful and immensely meaningful life. Chastity allows a man to enjoy his wife and a woman to enjoy her husband. It celebrates beauty without worshiping it. Chastity destroys domination and transforms us into respectful self-givers.

Chastity builds us in spirit, so we can look past a person's skin and into his or her character, insight, and depth. Chastity—in marriage or outside of it—is the channel that keeps sex pure, healthy, fun, and meaningful. Chastity leads us to know the God who is behind—and the Source of—the lovely things in this creation.

Isn't this what you want? A quiet love with God and many strong, healthy relationships with others? I want to be chaste because I want to be free to have the kind of relationships that will sustain me through the years.

Seek the interior strength of chastity. You will grow toward becoming the person you want to be—a man or woman who is building healthy, mature, and respectful relationships with God and the people He has placed in your life.

CHAPTER TEN

POSITIVE POSSESSION
(GENEROSITY)

The man who thinks nothing of goods has freed himself
from quarrels and disputes. But the lover of possessions
will fight to the death for a needle.

JOHN CLIMACUS

SEVENTEEN HUNDRED YEARS AFTER MOUNT VESUVIUS EXPLODED,
raining ash and lava upon the petrified citizens of Pompeii,
archaeologists began working their way through the layers of ash to
uncover history's most famous ghost town. Finally, they came across
the first of many skeletons.

As the researchers meticulously excavated the ancient citizen,
they discovered coins grasped tightly in his frozen skeletal hands.

It was enough to give everyone pause.

Because the citizens of Pompeii had been quickly buried under
tons of very fine ash, researchers were able to create plaster casts
which showed the people virtually "flash frozen" in their last seconds
of panic. One cast showed a woman clutching jewels. Some priests
were found who, in their final act of life, had collected statues and
temple treasures in a cloth sack. A couple died with their gold, jewels,
and silver amassed beside them.

There were a few more noble finds: Some people were found
comforting each other, their arms frozen in a farewell embrace.

The polytheistic religion of the Pompeiians celebrated health,
wealth, and affluence,[1] and had little concern for morality or virtue.

Minus the gods, the valueless system of our society is chillingly similar. To me, there is no more stark picture of the futility of such a system than those skeletons clutching their coins and jewels.

As counter-cultural as it may seem, generosity is a virtue that's absolutely essential for a soul that wants to remain free and to grow in spiritual health. For the attitude we have toward our money and possessions reaches to the depths of us, to the very nature of our existence.

BALANCING TWO REALITIES

We cannot live without possessions. Just try to survive a Texas August or an Alaskan January without appropriate clothes and shelter.

Possessions are necessary, so it is not sinful to desire certain things. As Kreeft points out, in a truly biblical worldview, "things" are good and are declared so by God Himself, who is the master creator. Sin enters our hearts not when we begin desiring things, but when we desire them out of proportion to their true worth. When our desire for the created eclipses our desire for the Creator, then we have entered blatant idolatry. "Avarice is not . . . desire for temporal possessions as such, but the *immoderate* desire for them; for it is natural to man to desire external things *as means*, but avarice makes them into ends, into gods." Kreeft adds, "When a creature is made into a god, it becomes a devil."[2]

A devil indeed. One of the dangers of greed is that it often doesn't set off the alarms that other sins do. Most people don't misinterpret sexual temptation; they know what they're facing. The lure of greed and materialism is more subtle. C. S. Lewis warns, "Prosperity knits a man to the world. He feels that he is 'finding his place in it,' while really it is finding its place in him."[3]

Does this mean it's wrong for Christians to aspire after better things? Not necessarily. If someone is locked in a dead-end job and if family needs really aren't being met, complacency is a precarious pulpit to preach from. On the other hand, what freedom is gained by transforming yourself from a "wage slave" into an emotional prisoner of a luxury car or the servant of a huge mortgage?

This is the fine line we walk: Maturity demands that every adult reading this book handle money and possessions, yet material things are just waiting for a shelf in our heart to open up so they can lay an illegitimate claim there.

Where is freedom for the Christian? What is our protection? It's found in the Christlike attitude of generosity.

THE PULL

"Adrienne" walks into the convenience store, bypasses the chips and soda, and goes immediately to the counter. She plucks ten dollars from her wallet and signals to the woman behind the counter, talking on the telephone, that she wants to buy ten lottery tickets. The clerk nods and, still talking on the phone, takes Adrienne's money. She pushes a button and produces the tiny slips of paper, which she hands back to Adrienne. With a slight rush of hope, Adrienne slips them in her purse and leaves the store.

Deep in her heart, Adrienne knows she is not buying security. She's tossed out too many losing tickets to believe she'll win. What she *is* buying is the opportunity to be lost in a fantasy. For the next day and a half, she will dream about the ways winning the lottery will change her life — the new clothes, the new house, the new car. She may even dream about the charities she will give to.

Eventually the numbers will be drawn and Adrienne will not win. The greed that fed her soul will fade until the next lottery is held. And what, some might say, is the real harm? It's just a game.

But those hours Adrienne passed thinking "what if" will prove to be completely without worth. Utterly wasted. Worse than that, Adrienne has planted discontent in her soul, without a realistic plan or effort to change her situation.

God wants to give Adrienne, and each one of us, our life back. He wants to set us free from the domination of money and possessions. The virtue of generosity confronts our deep fears that we will not have *enough*. There are few actions more typically human than striving for material gain, and there are few actions more divine in nature than sacrificially parting with them.

In this the hermits made a spiritually devastating mistake. In the desert without shoes, sometimes even without clothes, it may perhaps seem that materialism couldn't have much of a foothold. But here's the deception. In the desert, there is nothing to buy, but there is also no chance to *give*.

The truth is, fulfillment comes in being vessels of the generous heart of God by giving of our wealth and substance. God didn't create the world as a "level" roulette wheel, where some get lucky and some don't, all by chance. The way He has created us and the way He has designed the nature of human fulfillment is such that "it is more blessed to give than to receive."[4] God made us this way. He says, "If you want your life back, *give it away.*"

It seems illogical, but it's true. Do you want your life back? Give it to God. Do you want contentment? Learn how to wisely give your money away.

To do this, we must let go of the false security and pride in ownership that possessions promise.

LETTING GO

How do we begin to let go of an unhealthy grip on finances and possessions? Here are some steps.

1. Realize that possessions over-promise and under-deliver

As a writer, I've had a chance to hobnob with some of the rich and famous. Some time ago, I spent two days with heavyweight boxing champion Evander Holyfield. Many wondered why he made a comeback to the ring. He had a 57,000 square foot mansion, more cars than he could drive in a day, a regulation baseball diamond, and acres of land.

The truth? Though Holyfield sensed a "call" to return, he also admitted that he was just plain bored. He had tried riding horses and motorcycles. He spent time teaching his kids to play sports. But after a few months, he felt as imprisoned by his boredom as most of us feel about balancing a paycheck and a mortgage payment.

Our souls hunger for meaning, and meaning isn't found in soft, self-centered living. Materialism promises more than it can deliver in the long-run because joy and contentment are inner realities that come or don't come to us independent of our external situation. I've met independently wealthy people who have very meaningful lives, but their meaning comes from things like family and faith. And there are incredibly wealthy people who are miserable and alone.

Money cannot buy our way out of emptiness or into fulfillment. We're more likely to buy our way into boredom.

2. Consider the temptations of wealth

Wealth can create new temptations, new challenges, and new trials in your life. Money can cause us to become proud and controlling. When you can literally build or kill an entire ministry based on whether you give or withhold your money, the temptation to use your power wrongly can be strong, just as not having enough money can tempt you to despair.

The Bible is explicitly clear in this regard: A person who views money as an end is brought into many temptations. Paul writes, "People who want to get rich fall into temptation and a trap and into many foolish and harmful desires that plunge men into ruin and destruction. For the love of money is a root of all kinds of evil. Some people, eager for money, have wandered from the faith and pierced themselves with many griefs."[5]

3. Adopt an eternal perspective

I met a man in New England whose life was radically changed when a coworker died. These men had worked for one of the most stable and famous companies in the United States. The firm paid well but demanded a lot from its workers.

"We gave our lives to the company," this New Englander explained. "They took care of us but expected us to organize our lives around our work. If we said no even once, we'd be taken off the track of promotion and kept in a vocational eddy for the rest of our careers. So we got to work early and stayed late."

The colleague who died was only in his late forties. His replacement was on the job early the next morning.

My friend was devastated. "No one from work even went to the guy's funeral. Because they didn't know his family, they figured it didn't matter. He gave his entire life to the company, but the company didn't miss a step—not a single step—once he died. It was as if he never existed."

We pour ourselves into enterprises and business, but all of that security and meaning pale in the face of death and ultimate realities. To be freed from the lure and false security of money, learn to think *eternally.* Grasping the reality of heaven is a great antidote to the soul-poison of materialism.

4. Experience the internal joy of giving

Proverbs states, "A generous man will himself be blessed" (22:9). It might not make sense, but it's just the way God made this life work: "Give, and it will be given to you. A good measure, pressed down, shaken together and running over, will be poured into your lap."[6]

The joy of giving comes from taking on the attitude of Christ, who told us, "Freely you have received, freely give."[7] When we take on His character, we experience His presence.

But giving is about far more than money. It is a matter of character.

Spiritual Generosity

"Jane" walked into the party silently pleading, "notice me." She was plagued by worries about whether her hair was too flat, her makeup was too heavy, or her shoes didn't match her dress.

"Katie" entered the same party, asking God, "Is there someone I can serve tonight?" She soon found a newly divorced woman in need of a listening ear.

When you enter a gathering to receive, you put your fulfillment on the precarious pedestal of public opinion. When you seek to give, you're virtually assured of success, for there is always someone in need of care.

Material generosity is just the start of inner freedom. There is a spiritual generosity as well, a disposition that leads us to give and serve rather than crave to receive. The Spirit of Christ leads us into service and motivates us to allow God to reorient our motivations.

When I first started speaking and teaching in churches, I wanted a revival to start on the spot. It was important for me to hear, "Gary, that was really profound." "You're a fantastic speaker." "That's one of the best sermons I've ever heard."

It's humiliating to admit, but it was true. I had "small man's disease"—I spoke because I needed to be validated. My sermon preparation was not substantially different, morally, from the vain primping some people go through so their looks can wow people in public.

The change in me came from a divine challenge. As I was praying for an event a number of years ago, I sensed God telling me just to love the people I'd be speaking to. What I said was important, but giving myself to them was even more important.

It was a liberating weekend. I now know there's a tremendous difference between a teacher who wants to impart something important because he cares for his audience and one who wants to make a great impression.

After God reoriented my motivation, I became "addicted" to the joy and fulfillment of giving. Giving brings meaning to life and sets us free from the tyranny of vanity and egocentric living.

When you arrive at church on Sunday, are you there to give or to receive? When you show up for work, are you looking for others to notice you, or are you looking to notice others? When you arrive home from work, do you expect your family to circle the wagons around you, or do you pray, as one of my friends does, "Lord, give me the strength to be completely present with my wife and children"?

If your aim is to receive, you're going to be disappointed most of the time. We live in a world that is much too preoccupied with itself to pay others much attention. If your aim is to give, if you find your enjoyment in encouraging others, you will never want for fulfillment; there will always be plenty to give.

If you're stuck in the prison of bitterness and resentment because others don't appreciate or notice you, the virtue of generosity is the key to unlock your prison cell. Get your life back.

Let God teach you how to give.

CHAPTER ELEVEN

AWAKENED LIVING
(VIGILANCE)

Watch your life and doctrine closely.
1 TIMOTHY 4:16

"PAUL" AND "SUSAN" FACED THE FINANCIAL COUNSELOR AND sighed.

"You don't *know* how much you owe?" he asked.

"Not really."

"I want you to go home, add up everything you owe, and come back with a total."

That evening, the couple started punching numbers into the calculator with trepidation. The final total was staggering: $52,721.

"How did we get here?" Susan asked tearfully.

Paul shook his head. "I don't know."

The real problem behind their situation lies in Paul's admission: "I don't know." The Bible calls us to thoughtful living in which we pay attention to our spiritual health and external responsibilities. Our money won't manage itself. Relationships need to be cared for. Passion for God must be nurtured. Concern for the lost needs to be fed.

Traditionally, this careful attention has been called the virtue of *vigilance*. To be vigilant is to live with a mindfulness about life, your own attitudes, and your actions. Scripture encourages us to live a thoughtful and reflective life: "Only be careful, and watch yourselves closely so that you do not forget the things your eyes have seen or let them slip from your heart as long as you live."[1]

One of the most cherished promises of the Bible, given to David commends vigilance: "If your descendants *watch how they live*, and if they walk faithfully before me with all their heart and soul, you will never fail to have a man on the throne of Israel."[2] Perhaps that's why David is careful to promise, "I will watch my ways."[3]

Among Jesus' last words to His disciples were these: "*Watch* and pray so that you will not fall into temptation."[4] And many of Christ's teachings were punctuated with this call to vigilance: "Watch out! Be on your guard against all kinds of greed."[5] "Watch out that you are not deceived."[6]

We live in a complex and challenging world in which vigilance is essential. J. C. Ryle warns young men, "This world is not a world in which we can do well without thinking, and least of all do well in the matter of our souls."[7]

DAMNED FOR LACK OF THINKING

The Christian who understands vigilance of spirit is the one who recognizes there is more going on in his or her heart than he or she may realize. He thinks family tensions are under control. He assumes that the boss's harsh reaction, or his financial situation, or his friend's bad choices don't affect him. But they do.

Vigilance is the attitude that allows the Holy Spirit space and time to show us what's really going on inside us. "The vigilant [Christian] is a fisher of thoughts," John Climacus writes, "and in the quiet of the night he can easily observe and catch them."[8] So strong and rich in spirit is the man who understands his own soul that Climacus describes the process of vigilance as "collecting wealth."[9]

I like this last image because it removes vigilance from sounding so much like yet another obligation and presents it to us as the gift it is.

A gift? Yes, vigilance will sometimes show us we've sunken into a habitually bad mood or slipped into a terrible attitude. Sometimes we'll see how we've been actively courting temptation or have become overcommitted. Vigilance helps us assess the truth about our lives, so we can turn from our weaknesses and find divine help.

Thoughtful living is a tremendous opportunity with eternal implications. As Ryle points out, "Lack of thought is one simple reason why thousands of souls are cast away forever. Men will not consider, will not look forward, will not look around them, will not reflect on the end of their present course, and the sure consequences of their present ways, and awake at last to find they are damned for lack of thinking."[10]

When spiritual matters are involved, failing to give due caution can be eternally fatal.

THE ENEMY OF OUR SOUL

When I lived in Virginia, I spent a good bit of time visiting Civil War battlefields. I liked to pause at the little camps that marked where generals met with their subordinates to plot the next day's battle. These camps might be nothing more than a rock outcropping, but standing on that same patch of earth was still sobering. There's something particularly moving about the intense, quiet plotting that precedes the loud business of war.

The Christian classics frequently present this life as a war. We can't take hit after hit without spending some time regrouping. We need to be re-equipped and re-energized. We need to consider our next move. This is especially true as we become serious about our faith because our enemies will take notice.

In 1997, the Chicago Bulls were soundly defeating the Atlanta Hawks when Atlanta coach Lenny Wilkins sent in Eldridge Recasner, known for his three-point play-making ability. Recasner did his job, immediately hitting two three-pointers.

The next time he came down the floor, he looked up and saw Michael Jordan guarding him. "What are you doing here?" Recasner asked.

Michael didn't smile. He simply responded, "I'm here to stop you."

Recasner missed four of his next five shots.

The more serious you are about becoming a mature Christian, the more the war will intensify around you. John Climacus explains it this way: "War against us is proof that we are making war. . . . When a man is just a private citizen, a sailor, a laborer on the land, the enemies of the King do not take up arms against him. But when they see him accept the King's seal, the shield, the dagger, the sword, the bow, the uniform of a soldier, then they gnash their teeth and do all they can to destroy him. So let us not be caught napping."[11]

It sounds almost antiquated to talk about the Devil's work today. In our "enlightened" culture we've moved beyond the work of Satan. Yet Jesus and His apostles provide frequent warnings about the fact that we have a spiritual enemy.[12]

The Christian classics provide equal testimony to the work of Satan. John Owen calls vigilance "a moral sensitivity to the weakness and corruption within us." He warns that "we need to recognize the evil of sin and the power of temptation to work against us. If we remain careless and cold, we shall never escape its entanglements. We need to constantly remind ourselves of the danger of the entry of temptation."[13]

Owen laments that "it is sad to find most people so careless about this. Most people think about how to avoid open sin, but they never think about the dynamics of temptation within their hearts."[14]

Some of us, sad to say, pay less attention to our spiritual state than Satan does. As J. C. Ryle wrote, "You may be careless about your soul; [the Devil] is not."[15] Owen adds, "When we realize a constant enemy of the soul abides within us, what diligence and watchfulness we should have!"[16]

One morning as I prayed, I had the distinct impression the Holy Spirit was directing me to examine what was happening in my inner man. God brought to mind what I had watched on television the night before, the book I currently was reading, the schedule I was living, and all of it was placed together in context. I was picking up attitudes from all these sources that were less than godly. Though no single element was enough to cause serious spiritual trouble, all of them working together were weakening some of my important resolves.

I wouldn't have come to this conclusion on my own, and that's the good news: We are not left alone to accomplish the task of being vigilant over our own souls. Just as we have an unseen enemy, so we have in the Holy Spirit a present friend and protector who provides us with the insight we need.

DIVINE INSIGHT

The only thing sitting between me and Evander Holyfield was a small tape recorder and a pile of papers. We were sitting in his kitchen when the phone rang.

Holyfield was negotiating with Mike Tyson's camp for their first bout, but before Holyfield got up to answer the phone, he did something no other celebrity has ever done to me.

He reached over and turned off my tape recorder.

People who are used to working with the media have usually been burned so many times that they simply don't take a chance. They're vigilant. If they can't guard every word that comes out of their mouth — and that's difficult to do during a spontaneous phone call — they don't want a definitive record of the conversation.

If we gave as much consideration to our spiritual state as Holyfield gives to a reporter's tape recorder, we'd be doing well.

Christian vigilance is not just about self-examination. You could read a business book or a psychologist's self-help book to learn how to do that. Christian vigilance involves a plea for divine revelation, for someone outside ourselves to show us the truth about what's going on in the sometimes murky depths of our soul. We cannot trust our own insight or lean on our own understanding; we need to acknowledge God.[17]

Jeanne Guyon stresses the importance of making vigilance a predominantly divine activity: "It is not *your* diligence, it is not *your* examination of yourself that will enlighten you concerning your sin. Instead, it is God who does all the revealing. . . . If you try to be the one who does the examining, there is a very good chance that you will deceive yourself."[18]

When I find myself in conflict with someone, I can usually back up every disappointment I feel with tangible illustrations that could "prove" the accuracy of my complaint in a court of law. But in the silence of the dawn, God has the nerve to point the finger at *me*. God has the gall to suggest that I'm masking disappointment I feel in myself. *I'm* letting things slide. *I'm* forgetting to walk by faith. *I'm* the one dodging God's presence.

The beauty of divine vigilance as opposed to self-awareness is twofold. First, every rebuke I've ever received from God actually ends up encouraging me. I don't know how He does it, but God can take me to the spiritual woodshed, yet I end up walking back into the house feeling like God's favored son. That's the way God is.

Second, we live in an age of psychobabble and self-deceiving muck. God's vigilance is sharp. It cuts through the excuse language and seizes us by the heart. We want to pawn off the blame for our behavior on all the people who ignored us, abused us, and traumatized us. God wants us to experience the cleansing of repentance, and He zeroes in on our real motivations. True, we can always reject the truth, but we can no longer pretend we don't know the truth.

This is what the devil fears. Lewis's Screwtape speaks again: "It is funny how mortals always picture us as putting things into their minds; in reality our best work is done by keeping things out."[19]

THE PRACTICE OF VIGILANCE

Vigilance means ordering our outside world in such a way that we can nurture our inner world. It means we make spiritual health a significant factor in every decision. Ryle writes, "No place, no employment is good for you, which injures your soul. No friend, no companion deserves your confidence, who makes light of your soul's concerns."[20]

I've found it helpful to build little rituals into my life that remind me of the call to vigilance. Morning Scripture reading is a good one. It sets me in that reflective, listening mode right away.

A morning or afternoon commute to work, twenty minutes spent cleaning the kitchen, driving the kids to soccer or ballet practice— each of these can be turned into spiritual opportunities for vigilance. "Keep in view, morning, noon, and night, the interests of your soul. Rise up each day desiring that it may prosper; lie down each evening inquiring of yourself whether it has really made progress."[21]

What I believe Ryle is suggesting here is that we use the natural rhythms of life to keep our souls in check. Vigilance is a subtle but definite state of mind, cultivated in many short times of prayer— moments in which we ask, "God, what's going on?"

I call this "just checking in." After a speaking engagement, after a tough confrontation, after a battle of wills with a child, I like to tune in to God and say, "What's Your perspective on this?"

Thomas Kelly expresses this dynamic by urging us to live on two levels. "There is a way of ordering our mental life on more than one level at once," he writes in his classic, *A Testament of Devotion.* He urges us to bring all affairs before God and adds, "Facts remain facts when brought into the Presence in the deeper level, but their value, their significance, is wholly realigned."[22]

This means that we're listening for the truth beyond facts: We're listening for motivation, understanding, and a new perspective. This frees us from the trap of trying to be found right and instead focuses our attention on being a reconciler, a healing presence, and a prophetic soul.

I want to issue a caution: The attitude of vigilance is a tool to set us free and keep us free in spirit so that we can love, enjoy, and serve God. It is not meant to make us neurotic, religious messes. We can live in the loving, transforming presence of God and learn how to become more aware of what's going on inside and around us without guilt or condemnation.

Vigilance is a tremendously important virtue for Christians who live in the real world. It is a gutsy virtue, enabling men and women to courageously face both themselves and the grace of God honestly as they enter the glorious pursuit of life in Christ.

CHAPTER TWELVE

REALISTIC EXPECTATIONS
(PATIENCE)

Learn to suffer with patience. God will send frequent
and probably great suffering into your life. This is His doing;
He has chosen it; accept it.
JEANNE GUYON

THE SPORTS UTILITY VEHICLE PULLED UP TO THE CURB BESIDE THE
library. I saw the passenger side door open, and a gangly twelve-year-old boy flopped out of the car, leaving the door open as he ran a stack of books toward the library's book return slot.

It was a typical Virginia summer day, hot and humid, and the lazy air was soon shattered by a father's angry voice. "Can't you close the _____ door? You're going to break the _____ air conditioning!"

The book return was maybe fifteen feet from the curb and the boy had run the distance, meaning that he had left the car door open for about ten seconds, but it was enough to send his father off on a sweltering tirade. I have no idea how leaving the door open for that length of time could possibly "break" the air conditioning.

What must it be like to live with such anger, either as the perpetrator or the receiver? And what must this man be like when someone genuinely tries his patience? I couldn't tell how old he was, but I imagined him dying and clutching his chest. I also could imagine the boy's ambivalent feelings at the funeral.

Just go to a shopping mall and watch how irritably people can treat each other. God is offering you a way to avoid that. He will give you the spiritual power to extend grace and patience toward others. You can replace the bitterness of judgments, condemnations, and anger with an attitude that leads to patience. It just might save your life.

The heart journal *Circulation* published a study in late 1996, demonstrating that men with increased anger more than tripled their risk of heart attacks and coronary heart disease.[1] Drs. Redford and Virginia Williams put it succinctly: "Anger kills. We're speaking here not about the anger that drives people to shoot, stab, or otherwise wreak havoc on their fellow humans. We mean instead the everyday sort of anger, annoyance, and irritation that courses through the minds and bodies of many perfectly normal people. [Under the wrong conditions] getting angry is like taking a small dose of some slow-acting poison . . . every day of your life."[2]

THE BIRTH MOTHER OF IMPATIENCE

The birth mother of impatience—unfulfilled desires—is exposed by the apostle James: "What causes fights and quarrels among you? Don't they come from your desires that battle within you? You want something but don't get it."[3]

Impatience is an addiction to comfort, ease, and our own will. If we're late driving to the post office, we want every other driver out of our way. If we have a headache, we want those around us to intuit this and speak softly. We even want the weather to fit itself around our planned recreation.

Anger is born when we store impatience over time. A child may be shocked when a mother loses her composure over a pair of shoes left in the middle of the floor, but that child doesn't understand the irritation that's been seething for months. The mother isn't exploding over a single act but over a slow-burning series of events in which she perceives that the family takes her for granted.

Others of us poison ourselves at work, demanding unrealistic scenarios in our vocations. Not long ago I completed a cover story for a national magazine and felt very satisfied with the result.

When writing stories of this type, I often run draft copies past the people I interview so they can double-check their quotes. One man read what he had said and asked me to omit the most salient points of the interview. He suggested I replace his quotes with an awful alternative that read like an academic paper.

I was crushed, slumped before my computer and trying to salvage the article when Lisa saw my face and winced.

"All right, what are you depressed about?" she asked.

Is it that obvious? I thought.

It was. Something so minor as a blown interview can send me into a rotten mood. Why? My attachment to ease is passionate. I was focused on all the trouble I had yet to face, but the entire situation could have been looked at differently. So what if I had to ask the professional to reconsider? It might be unpleasant, but it wouldn't kill me. So what if I had to interview someone else? Maybe an even better article might result. So what if I had to work a little longer? That's a normal part of vocational life.

But my attachment to comfort blinded me to these things, and I let myself become irritated and depressed.

All sorts of events can hit us this way.

Being an at-home mom, with little kids who have no concept of schedule and who fight, or cry, or demand things all day long, can irritate your desire for peace and order. Working for a corporation mired in mindless bureaucracy, where the wrong people get hired for the wrong jobs, can be enormously frustrating.

Life involves many conflicts. It is unrealistic, unhealthy, and spiritually suicidal to live life expecting everything to fall into place just for you.

Life doesn't get out of the way simply because we become Christians. The sooner we accept this, the sooner we can begin to enjoy the benefits of patience.

SPIRITUALIZED IMPATIENCE

Even the way we "do" Christianity betrays how much our will is in the way. If we're going to grow in Christlikeness, we want maturity *now*. One decision, one trip to the altar for a prayer and public commitment, and we want it over and done with.

What we fail to understand is that our hard-won struggles are the ones that go deep. By definition, struggle isn't easy. In fact, struggle often involves defeat—or at the very least, severe setbacks. But it's the *process* that reveals deeper truths about us, and working all the way through the process of change will bring a more glorious end. "Good and blessed is that simplicity which some have by nature," says John Climacus, "but better is that which has been goaded out of wickedness by hard work."[4]

I knew a young man who had been a habitual cocaine user. God miraculously delivered him during a revival service, and soon he became enthusiastic for God. He didn't touch cocaine for an entire year. As the religious high began to fade, however, he started using crack again.

I remember looking him in the eyes and saying, "God gave you a tremendous gift, completely removing your craving for cocaine, but it may not be nearly so easy the second time. The next time, God is likely to ask you to walk out of addiction rather than catapulting you out of it."

While our natural tendency is to seek quick spiritual fixes, internally-based change usually lasts much longer. What we need, ironically enough, is to be patient with ourselves as we learn patience.

Climacus writes, "I cannot say why it is that some people appear to be naturally inclined to [be mild-mannered]. Others have to fight hard against their own natures to acquire these, they have to force themselves on to the best of their ability, suffering occasional defeat on the way; and it seems to me that the very fact of having to struggle against their own natures somehow puts them into a higher category than the first kind."[5]

How do we grow in patience?

THE MECHANICS OF PATIENCE

The first step in learning to practice patience is accepting discomfort. Paul urges us to be "patient in affliction."[6] The growth of every virtue begins when we accept with humility what God allows to come our way.

This does not mean merely putting a lid on our anger and resentment; it means crucifying our anger through the virtues of surrender and detachment. When I was back in Virginia and faced my fifth consecutive day suffering from sinus congestion as the skies pressurized for the next thunderstorm, I reminded myself that this is the life God has chosen for me. No, I won't get much work done this afternoon.

No, I won't be the life of the party with my kids. But this is the body God has given me. This is the climate in which God has placed me, and I need to accept it for now.

Since patience is born in acceptance and surrender, we have to be ruthless with our complaining. "Put to death the disagreeable feelings which rise up inside of you when unpleasant things enter your life."[7] Don't entertain immature, unrealistic expectations. They're wrecking your life. If you want your life back, you've got to rid yourself of fantasy.

Second, we need to practice the discipline of forgiveness. Paul tells Timothy that Christ's patience is "unlimited."[8] Think about that: *unlimited* patience. There's no breaking point with God. There's no, "I've had it with you employees!" Why? God forgives us and lets us start over. Impatience erupts when we hang on to the past.

Third, build a pause into your reactions, giving you time to do the all-important soul work of examining your motivations and desires. The man who blows up when his wife's problem can't be solved right away may not want a relationship with a real human being. Maybe he wants a Barbie doll or a mommy who never brings problems to him, only pleasure and help. If he can see the ridiculousness of his heart's demand, he can surrender it as unreasonable.

The woman who is angry at God for not healing her child's chronic illness needs to understand that she may be struggling against an unchangeable thing. Yes, by all means, pray and fast for healing! But if healing doesn't come, she may need to accept the fact that God's will can be done in other ways over time. Her focus can then shift to having (and promoting in her child) the inner peace and strength that brings spiritual victory out of physical weakness.

Beneath all this lies the need for wisdom. Proverbs 19:11 tells us, "A man's wisdom gives him patience; it is to his glory to overlook an offense." This means that we can allow Christ's patience to shine through us when we better understand the nature of the world—that it is a place of disappointment and failure, a fallen existence in which things go wrong every day. By reminding ourselves of this fact, we become less surprised and therefore less annoyed when things go wrong.

Wisdom includes maintaining an eternal perspective. The writer of Hebrews says, "We do not want you to become lazy, but to imitate those who through faith and patience inherit what has been promised."⁹ A patient Christian looks for satisfaction and freedom from irritation in the *next* world. Impatience arises when we begin seeking all the ease of heaven here on earth. God will certainly reward us, but some of us must learn to wait patiently—even until heaven, in some cases—to see it.

To enter the blessedness of patience is, in fact, to turn from wanting the world to love, cherish, and be kind toward us and to fall more deeply in love with God. "Learn to suffer all that happens to you—even confusion—but learn to do so out of only one motive: love for God."¹⁰ When a couple is on a date, infatuated and thrilled to be together, minor inconveniences become fun rather than traumatic. If they get caught in a downpour, they laugh. Their enjoyment of each other's company is such that the rest of life isn't nearly as important as the fact that they're facing it together.

God is offering you such an existence—a love relationship that won't shield you from trouble but will never leave you alone and powerless in that trouble. This is your inheritance as a Christian. We're told in Revelation that "patient endurance" is "ours in Jesus."¹¹ This is what God wants to give us, how He plans to rescue our life from this world. He hasn't promised to shield us from all persecution, disappointment, and pain. But He has promised to walk through it with us so that the persecution, disappointment, and pain make our spirits stronger.

Learning to walk in fellowship with God, in the patient spirit of Christ, will turn our irritable souls into sanctuaries of peace, where the quiet glory of Emmanuel—God in us—steadily shines.

Allow God to create more holy space in your heart by growing in the virtue of patience.

CHAPTER THIRTEEN
PURE PERCEPTION
(DISCERNMENT)

Hell itself is truth known too late.

J. C. RYLE

"YOU MUST LEARN TO READ MEN LIKE A BOOK."
The then-prime minister of Burma, U Nu, listened intently to the words spoken by Frank Buchman, leader of the Oxford Group (also known as Moral Re-Armament), a powerful Christian renewal movement that had a major impact on world events in the first half of this century. Buchman had a gift of calm grace, mixed with the ability to read men "like a book." And thus he had a profound impact on leaders around the world.

One of the richest men in India was startled while praying with Buchman. Abruptly, Buchman leveled his gaze at him and said the Lord had told him to say, "Stop stealing." The Indian man stormed out of the room . . . only to return the next day to confess, "I have been cheating the government on taxes for years."

A Chinese dissident leader called Buchman "the only man who told me the truth about myself." This was also the experience of a British colonel when he approached Buchman about a problem he was having with his son. He complained that though he prayed for his son, made him go to church, and taught him Bible verses, his son was still full of hate.

Buchman looked the colonel in the eye and said, "Have you been honest with your son about your own life? Have you told him what you were like at his age—and what you are like today?"

The father protested, "That would never do. It would embarrass the boy. We don't do that sort of thing in England," to which Buchman replied that the father might be more embarrassed than the son, and that his pride might mean more to him than giving the boy what would help him most.[1]

Witnessing such clear-sighted discernment into what is really going on inside people's souls can be unnerving. But there is ample evidence in Scripture and Christian history that holiness awakens every fiber of our being, including that element commonly referred to as *discernment*. The presence of Christ gives us a clearer eye with which to see the truth about people and situations, providing rare insight.

Jonathan Edwards writes, "The child of God is graciously affected because he sees and understands something more of divine things than he did before."[2] In this, Edwards merely echoes the psalmist: "You, through Your commandments, make me wiser than my enemies. . . . I have more understanding than all my teachers, for Your testimonies are my meditation. I understand more than the ancients, because I keep Your precepts" (Psalm 119:98-100, NKJV).

Edwards explains, "There is an understanding of divine things which in its nature and character is wholly different from all knowledge that natural men have."[3]

Spiritual understanding comes from adopting God's view of all things. God understands our motivations, our fears, and our longings. He also knows how the world is meant to work—the importance of relationships over possessions, commitment over excitement, the eternal over the temporal. When we truly know God, listen to Him, and are conformed to His image, He reveals these insights to us.

Climacus describes discernment as "a solid understanding of the will of God in all times, in all places, in all things; and it is found only among those who are pure in heart, in body, and in speech."[4] This understanding seeks to cultivate the intellect with the wisdom of God. It doesn't result in new doctrines or esoteric explanations of parables—God's wisdom doesn't change—but it does create an excellence of understanding and perception.

Jesus had this quality about Him. The Bible says people were amazed at Christ's teaching because He taught as one who had authority.[5] His words shot into the human heart and revealed something people had never seen or heard before. We like to focus on the miracles Jesus performed, but even more fascinating to me is His fertile mind.

How can we grow in this quality of Jesus?

APPREHENDING SPIRITUAL BEAUTY

One time I boarded a small commuter airplane and was assigned a seat directly across the aisle from a very attractive woman. I was the last person off the plane, so on my way to the baggage claim, I surveyed the reactions of the men in the airport as this woman walked down the hall.

Sometimes, a man's casual glance would be followed by a quick jerk back and then a long piercing stare. Other men would not be quite so bold. They kept turning their heads — a quick look at the woman, followed by a quick nervous glance back at their wives.

Three skycaps rammed their carts against each other in an attempt to ask the woman if she needed help.

You know what? This woman might be a bear to live with — demanding, selfish, and cruel. Or perhaps she is incredibly kind and thoughtful. Nobody watching her had a clue, but that didn't matter because beauty, in and of itself — even, unfortunately, apart from character — arrests us.

The beauty of God is even more powerful than humankind's reflection of beauty, because God is not just beautiful — He is beauty itself. And just as men will do silly things to attract a beautiful woman, so we will do radical things to live in obedience to a beautiful God — if, that is, our eyes are opened to His beauty. Grasping the beauty of God is thus key to holiness and discernment.

Jonathan Edwards says spiritual understanding begins with this sense of "spiritual beauty." "For whoever does not see the beauty of holiness cannot appreciate the graces of God's Spirit. Without this there is ignorance of the whole spiritual world."[6]

If someone cannot perceive light, he is blind. Light is a basic component of sight, so if you can't see it, you really can't see anything. In the same way, God's beauty is the basic component of spiritual understanding and insight. If we miss that, we miss the spiritual shapes and contours that really matter, and we get used to, or even become enamored of, a fallen world with its skewed angles. We'll value what we shouldn't value; we'll treat with contempt what is most precious. This is what Jesus was talking about when He said, "The eye is the lamp of the body. If your eyes are good, your whole body will be full of light. But if your eyes are bad, your whole body will be full of darkness. If then the light within you is darkness, how great is that darkness."[7]

Spiritual beauty creates the context for our obedience, and it serves to refine our spiritual taste so that valuing what God values, seeing things His way becomes a passion and joy, rather than a legalistic obligation.

REFINED TASTE

How do we apprehend this beauty?

Buchman once offered some practical advice to a young man who brought tea to his room. "You have to get to the place where you prefer Him above all men and things. . . . Your heart has got to come alive . . . [to] prefer Him above all men and things. Shed every secondary motive.

"I streamlined my life long ago: 'Make and keep me pure within.' Pure within. No heart is pure that is not passionate."[8]

By "streamlining," Buchman means we remove anything that might challenge or block our love for God. In Buchman's view, "any relationship with any other person that is more important to you than your relationship with God—or theirs—has something wrong with it."[9] When God isn't first in our lives, then our priorities are out of whack and our understanding will be darkened accordingly.

How do you know if you're placing someone above God? Ask yourself these questions: Do you ever fail to speak the truth to someone because you fear his or her disapproval? This could include children, spouses, bosses, church members, boyfriends, and girlfriends. Are you prone to flattery? Are you willing to compromise on what is right if in doing so you win someone else's appreciation or affection, even while knowing that your actions are displeasing to God?

In addition to streamlining, Buchman was insistent on absolute purity. "It is amazing how these—I won't call them sins, I just call them nice little vices—can sometimes be the key to a man's whole life."[10] When we depend on sin to get through the day, we bend our heart away from God and lose sight of His beauty.

"[Buchman] saw clearly that the reason that so many Christians were well-meaning but powerless in the lives of their nations and even their families was because they professed Christ with their lips but compromised in their lives. He saw that any valid experience of faith carried deep moral change with it. He saw that those who professed faith but lived filth, denied before men the power of God as a force in their nature."[11]

Paul wrote in Romans, "For although they knew God, they neither glorified him as God nor gave thanks to him, *but their thinking became futile and their foolish hearts were darkened.*" Then they lapsed into immorality.[12]

Biblically, there is a connection between immorality and stupidity, lack of understanding, and denseness. When we don't revel in God's glory, acknowledge His superiority, greatness, and beauty, we spurn the standard by which every human action, thought, and deed must be measured.

If we are captivated by God, something that opposes God will begin to repel us, making holiness, quite literally, a matter of taste. Edwards explains, "If an unworthy or unholy action is suggested to the spiritually discerning, a sanctified eye sees no beauty in it nor is pleased with it. Sanctified taste will only be nauseated by it. In this way a holy person is led by the Spirit by having a holy taste and disposition of heart."[13]

My son came to me one day and said, "Here Dad, try this piece of candy." I popped the candy into my mouth and it exploded into the most sour-tasting assault you could imagine. Graham doubled over in laughter. "It's a Mega-Sour Warhead!" he shouted, giggling all the while. I didn't have to think about what to do. Instinctively, I spit that candy *out*.

"Don't throw it away!" Graham shouted, horrified. "Give it to me! I'll eat it!"

As our spiritual taste is refined, we will react to sin like I reacted to that candy. This is why it's so important to focus on building the inner life instead of relying on outer discipline. Just as you'll scrunch your nose if you get a whiff of sour milk, so your spirit will cringe when you come across sin—if you've done the inner work we've been talking about in this book.

The good news is, taste can be cultivated. I grew up with incredibly poor taste in food. I then married a woman who thinks anything that doesn't actually grow out of the ground can't be considered real food. We drove by a McDonald's on our honeymoon, but when I suggested we stop there, Lisa was perplexed. "I'm hungry," she said. "And they don't have anything to eat there."

McDonald's does billions of dollars worth of business a year—somebody is finding something to eat there. But by my wife's refined standards, there was nothing she could imagine ordering. Just as I can learn to like broccoli and salad because vegetables are better for me than brownies, so I can cooperate with the Holy Spirit to see my spiritual taste gradually transformed and inclined toward greater holiness.

EXPERIENCE

A third component of discernment is *experience*. Our faith is based on truth, not experience, but our wisdom grows only in experience. Jonathan Edwards understood this truth. In speaking of the early martyrs, he observed, "The . . . martyrs of Jesus Christ [were] not merely those who strongly believed the gospel of Christ is true. They [saw] the truth for themselves."[14]

In other words, they experienced it.

As we experience the reality of Christ, the beauty in living by God's wisdom and ways, something transforming happens in us. We gradually stop becoming mere religious critics, faultfinders, and sin spotters. We become, instead, discerners of the hidden motives that bind men's hearts to sin and make their lives weak, mean, and miserable.

Do we want to present Christ to the world, or merely rules? Young people will not quit sexual activity outside of marriage simply because we can make a compelling argument for how such an action assaults character. A married couple contemplating a divorce will not likely respond to eloquent sermons on how the disintegration of marriage is ruining our society. Such self-denial needs a full heart arrest to become effectual, as well as enlightened logic. If we want a relevant ministry, we must be able to pass on *experience*.

In his autobiography, jazz musician Miles Davis recalls an enchanting introduction to the soul of jazz the first time he heard Charlie Parker and Dizzy Gillespie play. The musical form these men perfected influenced Davis for the rest of his life. "I've come close to matching the feeling of that night in 1944 in music . . . but I've never got there," he writes. "I'm always looking for it, listening and feeling for it, though, trying to always feel it in and through the music I play everyday."[15]

Watching Diz and Bird, Miles Davis understood true jazz because he had experienced it. The same can be true of spiritual experience. I've done quite a bit of reading on the life of the great sixteenth-century Christian mystic, John of the Cross, and people's reactions to him were remarkably similar. They said that, above all else, John *made Christ real* to them. Somehow, when John of the Cross spoke, Christ's presence was translated through his words. John's listeners weren't just dealing with principles or stories; a deeper part of them was touched, eternity was opened just a little, and they tasted a supernatural presence.

You can read all about jazz, but until you hear it, it remains only a concept, one of many possible musical forms. You can read about the spiritual life, but until you experience it, its grip on your heart will be tenuous at best. People are looking for true spiritual experience. This is where a church, a community of people who are "fleshing out" the gospel and translating theory into reality, becomes so essential.

This genuineness of experience is what usually becomes so evident when someone is teaching. When holiness is a concept instead of a passion, and God is a force instead of the soul's love, the words we hear are weak and lifeless. Somehow, our soul senses instinctively when a teacher is genuinely grappling with the truth being taught, and it makes all the difference in the world.

Just imagine being someone's "spiritual" Charlie Parker or Dizzy Gillespie. Imagine what it would be like if, after someone met you, he was influenced for the rest of his life. I can imagine nothing more rewarding than to so experience the light of Christ that others sense Him, even in the smallest way, in my living, in my treatment of them, and in my words.

SPIRITUAL MUSCLE

When we gain wisdom, our mind becomes an instrument of holy war, a spiritual muscle. Jesus is the One who elevated the role of the mind in the Christian life. The Pharisees would have been delighted to limit virtue to bodily activities, but Jesus put lustful fantasies on a par with lustful deeds.[16] He compared the murderous thought with the murderous act.[17]

God has given us something animals don't have—moral understanding. We are not slaves to our darker inclinations. We can sift through the options that lie before us and say, "No, I will reject that because it is not in line with the beautifully holy life God offers me."

Our oldest daughter used to run and grab our youngest daughter from behind—not with malice, but in play. Even so, the grab hurt our youngest and caused her to cry. We urged our oldest, "Think about what you're doing before you do it. Think about how this might scare a younger child. Think about the fact that you are stronger than she is and how you might accidentally squeeze too hard."

When I discern a clear temptation, I apply this same teaching to myself. Exercising my mind as a spiritual muscle, I remind myself *why* I need to respond in a holy manner. I think about my family, my reputation, my commitment to the Lord. I think about long-term spiritual fulfillment, building a life of meaning, and not offending the God who has shown me such mercy. I may meditate on a response of Christ to a similar temptation. This is part of what the Bible means by saying, "Resist the Devil, and he will flee from you."[18] Our resistance means exposing the Devil's lies, and we use our mind, in league with the light of God's Word, to do that.

Other biblical passages back this up. Peter told Christians to "prepare your minds for action."[19] Solomon said, "I turned my mind to understand, to investigate and to search out wisdom and the scheme of things and to understand the stupidity of wickedness and the madness of folly."[20]

Maintaining the mind of Christ is a choice that may involve considerable struggle. Sometimes, I have found that the mind of Christ is preserved only with a fierce determination: "I *will* set my mind on things above. I will *not* dwell on earthly things." Other times, it's a natural outpouring of God's current blessing.

But with the mind of Christ, I know I never go into spiritual warfare without being fully armed. Jesus, Peter, and Solomon are in agreement: Use your mind as a muscle. Exercise it. Live thoughtfully. Become wise beyond your years by adopting the knowledge of Scripture and then forcefully calling it into play.

THE COVERING OF DISCERNMENT

When something is new and exciting — a hobby, a relationship, a job — it's hard to get it out of your mind. You dream about it at night. You wake up thinking about it in the morning. It covers you.

Discernment covers our thoughts with the presence, beauty, and fellowship of Jesus Christ. We don't live an infatuated existence, but our hearts are perpetually "warmed up," ready to enjoy Jesus as He walks with us through the day. And the presence of Jesus is transforming. He refines our taste; puts "mental muscle" behind our commitment to be true to Him; unlocks valuable insights and wisdom; and leads us into rich experience.

The difference? You'll create more treasured memories than regrets. You'll look back on your days and have a quiet pleasure instead of a despairing dread. You'll make good, wise choices and experience a corresponding inner peace.

Don't you want this? Let God rescue you from skewed perceptions. Let Him remake you as a vessel of His beautiful, freeing truths. Ask Him to begin a new work in you today, healing your spiritual eyes and giving you the virtue of discernment.

CHAPTER FOURTEEN
EXUBERANT LIVING
(THANKFULNESS)

Grace always attendeth him that is truly thankful.
THOMAS À KEMPIS

WHEN PRO FOOTBALL HALL OF FAMER AND UNITED STATES Congressman Steve Largent watched his wife give birth to his fourth child, he was elated to see another son come into their family. Then the doctor said, "Uh-oh, we've got a problem," and Steve froze. His son was born with the exposed spinal cord condition, *spina bifida.*

As Steve wept, his wife, Terry, comforted him by saying, "God planned Kramer. Having him in our lives will be one of the greatest things that ever happened to us."

Today, Steve and Terry have found cause to be thankful in the face of a situation that would leave many parents angry and bitter. "For myself and for my wife, we wouldn't change a thing," Steve says. "For our son, we wish it would be different, that he didn't have to live with this. But having a child with a disability has added more to our lives than anything else. It's given us more compassion and sympathy for other couples facing difficult challenges."[1]

What is it that helps one person become thankful while another becomes bitter?

William Law, the eighteenth-century Anglican, asks an intriguing question: "Would you know who is the greatest saint in the world?" His answer is fascinating: "It is not he who prays most or fasts most. It is not he who gives the most money . . . but it is he who is always thankful to God, who wills everything that God wills, and who receives everything as an instance of God's goodness and has a heart always ready to praise God for it."[2]

Thankful Christians have cultivated a view of God's goodness in which they believe that He can work through all things. In humility, they're willing to accept that their understanding doesn't define God's goodness, so even when things look bad, they find something to be thankful for.

This is right in line with Scripture. First Chronicles 16:8 urges us to "Give thanks to the LORD." Ephesians 5:20 emphasizes this, saying we should "always [give] thanks to God the Father." First Thessalonians 5:18 is even more direct: "Give thanks in all circumstances."

Thankfulness is one of the most beautiful, and spiritually strengthening, attitudes of Christ. It is true that God deserves our thankfulness, but duty and obligation are hardly good motivators. Thankfulness, as an attitude, is like a fuel that powers the Christian life and keeps us moving on the pathway of spiritual growth, even when the climb is steep and the trail rough. Unless we learn how to cultivate a thankful heart, we become stuck in bitterness.

A PRIVILEGE

A number of years ago, I returned from a trip late at night. I was tired from the stress of being on the road, but as soon as I got home, my wife met me at the door with a recital of about four or five things that had broken while I was gone: A closet door was out of its track, a toilet wouldn't stop leaking, a refrigerator shelf had broken loose. . . .

"Stop!" I wanted to yell. "Just tell me what *isn't* broken so I can leave it alone."

The next morning I struggled inwardly as I hugged a toilet, trying to fit a wrench around a nut in the back. I began to grow bitter. I was tired. I wanted a day off. No, I *deserved* a day off. I could use a walk in the open air. I could be playing with the children. Instead, I was hugging a smelly porcelain bowl. The "I" statements poured out of me as fast as the water poured out of the back of the toilet.

Then I remembered how my wife and I had prayed for God to provide this house. I remembered how cold it had been outside and how nice it was to come into a place that was warm, though I must admit I cast a wary glance at the aging heat pump. I began thanking God for the benefit of space, protection from the weather, and a living room that my wife could decorate in a way that she loves doing.

I remembered when we used to live in an apartment with just one small child, and a neighborhood girl visited, her eyes bulging when she saw the small plastic kitchen set that belonged to our daughter. This little girl lived in a townhouse with three families. She couldn't believe how much space our daughter had to play in.

In short, I found things to thank God for, and my heart was drawn to God.

Wait a minute, you might interject — what about the reality of a terrible situation? Isn't thankfulness naive? In response, I'd like to pose a different question: Has an attitude of bitterness ever healed a disabled child? Filled a bank account? Repaired a car or a leaky toilet?

No, being thankful doesn't fix the broken lives or bitter losses. But it does transform our spirit as we face them. And since we will have to live through hardships in this fallen world, we need the power — the very great power — of a spirit that is at peace and even joyful to carry us through the toughness of life.

The virtue of thankfulness is power to the soul. God offers it to us to drive out the spiritually degenerative illness of bitter, negative thinking. I like to think of thankfulness as God's "spiritual air freshener." It replaces the stale odor of resentment with clean, fresh-smelling air for the soul to breathe.

CULTIVATING A THANKFUL HEART

My wife and I had been back in Washington state for less than two months. We were ecstatic about being back "home," but as we drove down I-5 to visit family, Lisa cast a speculative glance at the skies.

"It's so gray out here," she said. "Don't you ever miss the sun?"

I smiled, and Lisa read my mind. "Oh, great," she said. "I suppose you're just thankful that it's not raining for a change so you can drive on dry roads."

I laughed out loud. That's *exactly* what I was thinking. I've come to cherish the practice of looking for something to thank God for.

For me, it was no quick journey from being a constant complainer to becoming an active thanker. Several small but progressive steps led me onward. Each step was a little more difficult than the previous one, but each new one also produced an increased spiritual benefit.

I know you can find benefit in these steps, too, as you cultivate the spiritually empowering thankfulness of Christ.

1. Recognize the danger of not giving thanks

Paul warned us of a people who knew God but who failed to develop the discipline of thankfulness. The results were disastrous. "For although they knew God, they neither glorified him as God *nor gave thanks to him*, but their thinking became futile and their foolish hearts were darkened."[3] We referred to this verse in the previous chapter, but it's just as relevant here. When we're not thankful, we rob God of His glory, lose sight of His beauty, our hearts become darkened, and we lose perspective.

It's as dangerous for a Christian not to give thanks as it is for a driver to leave her seat belt disconnected. When accidents happen — and, eventually, they will — we'll be left unprotected. If we don't adopt thankfulness, we undermine our own spiritual stability by questioning whether God is, after all, a loving Father. The difficulty of our situation and even the frustration of relatively minor nuisances can cloud our spiritual vision and tempt us to reconsider spiritual absolutes that we know are true.

Time after time I've seen Christians facing difficulties. They need God's love in a desperate way, but they're too busy *accusing* Him to receive the confidence and strength they need. When I find my heart drifting toward resentfulness, I remind myself that it's spiritually dangerous to stop cultivating a heart of thankfulness.

2. Arm yourself with verses that call us to give thanks

I'm always impressed with people who know truths from the Bible by heart. The Word of God is what we need to renew our minds and to redirect it into a positive thought-flow.

The Bible is full of verses that call us to give thanks. In the Old Testament, we find beautiful truths about God, on which to fix our minds:

- 1 Chronicles 16:34: "Give thanks to the Lord, for he is good; his love endures forever."
- Psalm 69:30: "I will praise God's name in song and glorify him with thanksgiving."

From the New Testament, I particularly like these soul-directing truths:

- Ephesians 5:18-20: "Be filled with the Spirit . . . [give] thanks to God the Father for everything."
- Colossians 3:15: "Let the peace of Christ rule in your hearts. . . . And be thankful."

These verses, and many others, remind us of an important spiritual truth: While we cannot control our circumstances, we can control the lens through which we view them.

3. Thank God for the easy things

To begin seasoning my soul with thankfulness, I started with things that are easy to give thanks for: the beauty of the natural world, God's goodness in sending His Son to be my Savior, and the blessing of my family.

When life feels flat, and I don't *feel* thankful, I return to truth of Scripture, which directs me to invisible realities I can so quickly forget, such as Psalm 7:17, which says, "I will give thanks to the LORD because of his righteousness." I may be having a bad day, but does that mean God isn't righteous? I may lack the spiritual strength to thank God for the difficult day itself, but I can always thank Him for His righteousness and keep my soul from angling onto the wrong path.

Thanking God for the easy things helps me to redirect my focus. There comes a time when thinking about a problem loses its constructive nature and becomes fretting. When this happens, there is no better medicine for me than to take a break from my relatively small world and set my mind on higher things. For me, that can mean a walk on a wooded path, in nature's calming solitude. In prayer, I thank God for the beauty that's all around me. This is freeing, relaxing, and it returns me to the path of thankfulness toward God.

4. Thank God for the way He used difficult things in the past to build you up in the faith and make you a stronger person

I'll never forget that bald head. The man was probably still in his thirties, but I was nineteen years old at the time, and thirty-two seemed ancient. The two of us were battling it out for the lead in a six-mile road race. He had more speed; I had more strength. On the flats, he broke away. When we got to the hills, I caught him and then passed him.

My view of training changed that day. On training runs, as I'd approached the crest of a hill, I wondered why I was doing this to myself. My legs would have that weak, blown-out feeling; my lungs would burn. I thought, *Is the pain really worth it?*

But during this race, every time I saw my competitor fall back as we reached another incline, I was thankful for the times I'd endured training on the hills. In this case, because the finish line was at the top of a hill, I won the race.

The same principle holds true for my spiritual struggles. If God allows us to traverse only flat spiritual ground, our spiritual muscles won't strengthen. Perhaps it's too difficult to thank God for a hard struggle while you are right in it, but you can look back and say, "God, you really helped me mature during that last difficult time. Thank You."

5. Thank God for what He is doing through the hard things in your life today

Once you thank God for the easy things, it is possible to progress and begin thanking Him for the difficult things in the past. You'll soon find you are able to thank God for what He is doing through the difficult circumstances in the present. Remember, there's a difference between thanking God *for* the difficult things and thanking God *in* the difficult things. What exactly is the difference?

The answer for me came when I combined "giving thanks in all circumstances" with Romans 8:28-29: "And we know that in all things God works for the good of those who love him, who have been called according to his purpose. For those God foreknew he also predestined to be conformed to the likeness of his Son."

If we miss this, we miss everything. *It is God's will that we be conformed to the image of His Son.* Virtually any circumstance—however painful or pleasant—can be used by God to shape the character of Christ in me, and it is for that shaping we can be thankful.

The rub is that *my* purpose for me might be different from *God's* purpose. Steve Largent admitted he wished his son didn't have to suffer spina bifida. This is where the virtues of humility and surrender become coworkers with thankfulness to help us stay on course and maintain the right spirit.

This requires more than a glib, "Oh thank You, God," which does not require the soul-searching effort it takes to understand what motive He is working to replace in us. When my friend died of muscular dystrophy, I couldn't thank God for the loss of his friendship. I could, however, thank God for relieving Gordy from his suffering. I could also thank God that He had allowed one more event in this passing world to make me eager for heaven . . . where I'll see Gordy again, and where his approach won't be preceded by the whir of an electric wheelchair.

God knows best. It's impossible for me to dwell on such things and not become very thankful for a God who eventually defeats the worst diseases and even death itself.

6. Practice giving thanks

So much in this world pushes us to be disgruntled.

I sometimes lag in the practice of thankfulness and have to remind myself that giving thanks is a discipline. As an act of my will, I must choose to dwell on good things, on the high qualities of my invisible but ever-present Father. I consciously bend my thoughts away from resentment and remind myself I must wait for God to work out His best plans in due time.

Sometimes it helps me to pray prayers of thanksgiving out loud so I can hear the words of thankfulness. Once thankfulness becomes a habit, it takes on a life of its own and becomes a source of tremendous strength. My goal is to have my children hear me say "Thank You, God" many times every day. I've been around people who say "shoot!" and "darn it" and worse. I want my kids' memories to be burned with their father's frequent utterance of "Thank You, Lord." I want this because thankfulness is one of the surest paths to God and to a peace-filled spirit.

THE PATH TO GOD

"Here's some literature," the ophthalmologist said. "It'll explain your condition."

I thumbed through the booklet on my way out to my car. *Mourning?* I thought. *I'm supposed to go through a period of mourning?*

When I got home, Lisa took the booklet and started reading. "Gary, this is awful," she gasped.

One of my eyes has a degenerative disease. I noticed it a few years ago, when a book I was reading went fuzzy. Now, when I close my right eye, the world suddenly becomes blurry. This was a stunning blow to me, as I grew up with 20-20 eyesight. Now, even eyeglasses won't do a thing because my cornea is misshapen. Contact lenses won't work either, as they won't fit over my now oddly shaped eyeball. The only thing that would help is a cornea transplant.

Now, when my right eye is closed or night approaches, I suddenly resemble the cartoon character Mister Magoo. Once, I completely missed a turn on the road. "What are you, blind?" my wife called out, then caught herself and said, "Oh, honey, I'm so, so sorry. I didn't mean that. I was just—"

"Don't worry about it," I laughed. "I know what you meant."

The practice of giving thanks has led me to face this degeneration of an eye with an entirely different attitude than I would have had a number of years ago. There's nothing the doctors can do to stop the disease, but it bothers me very little. The reason for this state of grace within me is that I trust God. Whatever happens, I know He is going to use it, somehow, for His purposes. Fretting and bitterness will not heal my eye. But thanking God for all that He has done, is doing, and will do will be health to my spirit.

Henri Nouwen gave up a position at Yale University to work with developmentally disabled adults. Watching people who have been given some of the hardest lives to live taught him some profound lessons on gratitude. He's worth quoting at length:

"Where there is reason for gratitude, there can always be found a reason for bitterness. It is here that we are faced with the freedom to make a decision. We can decide to be grateful or to be bitter. . . .

"I see this every day in our community. The . . . men and women with mental disabilities have many reasons to be bitter. Many of them experience deep loneliness, rejection from family members or friends, the unfulfilled desire to have a partner in life, and the constant frustration of always needing assistance. Still, they choose mostly not to be bitter, but grateful for the many small gifts of their lives — for an invitation to dinner, for a few days of retreat or a birthday celebration, and most of all, for their daily life in community with people who offer friendship and support.

" . . . and [so] they become a great source of hope and inspiration for all their assistants who, although not mentally disabled, also have to make that same choice. . . . What fascinates me so much is that every time we decide to be grateful it will be easier to see new things to be grateful for. Gratitude begets gratitude, just as love begets love."

God uses the virtues of Christ to give us our life back, and in fact, to give us a higher experience of our human life in a very fallen world. Many are those who waste their lives worrying, mourning, or crying out in complaint — and nothing good will come of it.

For many of us, thankfulness starts out sounding shallow and trite. But the truth is, it leads us into a deeper journey with God than we imagined, taking us down to the core reason why we are here: to fulfill our own purpose for living — or His. "Enter his gates with thanksgiving," the psalmist wrote, "and his courts with praise; give thanks to him and praise his name."[4]

If I want to enter God's gates — and I do, with all my heart — it will only happen as God's spirit of thanksgiving enters me.

Thankfulness isn't an obligation; it's my privilege as a child of God. It is your key, and your privilege, too.

CHAPTER FIFTEEN

CARESSING LIFE
(GENTLENESS)

The Scripture speaks of no real Christian who has an ugly, selfish, angry, and contentious spirit. Nothing can be more contradictory than a morose, hard, closed, and spiteful Christian.

JONATHAN EDWARDS

I CHECKED THE CAR SEAT BUCKLE FOR THE THIRD TIME. ALLISON, our firstborn, was thirty-six hours old, and I was determined that she'd live for at least another eighty years.

The car seat was placed in the exact middle of the back seat, then I placed rolled up towels around Allison's body, just in case. I think a nuclear missile could have broadsided us, and Allison still would have had a 50-50 chance of survival.

We lived about three miles from the hospital, but I drove so slowly and cautiously that it took about fifteen minutes to get home. No telling how slippery the road might be on a perfectly dry, sunny spring day.

This was my first child, and nothing was going to harm her.

Some ten years later, I stand in a pool and hurl my children into the water, throwing them as high as I can. After more than a decade of child rearing, you realize kids aren't quite as fragile as they first appear. But I'll never forget the gentleness with which I treated our firstborn.

This is the same gentleness that Paul commands us to have toward others. He says that as apostles—as living examples of the character of Christ — "we were gentle among you, like a mother caring for her little children."[1]

Gentleness is so crucial to the Christian experience that Edwards suggests gentleness "may well be called the Christian spirit. It is the distinguishing disposition in the hearts of Christians to be identified as Christians. . . . All who are truly godly and are real Disciples of Christ have a gentle spirit in them."[2]

What is the attitude of Christ that gives us this gentle spirit? How do we become gentle in a brutal world?

THE TASKMASTER

"Gary, you're a lazy bum."

The person speaking was *me*. It was 10:00 P.M., and I'd just spent thirty minutes watching television. "What an absolute waste of time," I muttered to myself. "You have a serious discipline problem."

By the time I reached the top of the stairs, an inward nudge had arrested me. I was led to reconsider my day. I'd spent twelve hours at work, two hours commuting, and when I had gotten home, even though I was tired, I'd agreed to play "Chutes and Ladders" with my children.

Most parents know that "Chutes and Ladders" was designed as a cruel punishment for the well-meaning but gullible parents who buy it:

"Now, Daddy, do I go up the slide?"

"No, you go *down* the slide and *up* the ladder."

It can try a parent's patience like nothing else, especially at the end of a long day.

After we finished playing the game, I put the kids to bed and spent some time talking to Lisa.

As I re-evaluated my day, I saw that thirty minutes of watching television didn't erase a day's worth of service. In fact, I had made many good choices. Why was I so harsh with myself?

I don't think I'm an exception. Mentally, many of us flagellate ourselves over failure and embarrassments. Where does this self-attacking attitude come from?

A harsh view of God leads us to be brutal with ourselves and demanding with others. Many of us look upon God as sort of a celestial Mark Twain — brilliant, but not easy to work for. After reviewing the work of one proofreader, Twain called upon the full armament of his wit to reduce the poor fellow to a shrunken heap: "The man was an idiot," he said. "And not only was he an idiot, but he was blind. And not only was he blind, he was partly dead."

Some people think God treats us this way, ruthlessly demanding perfection and letting us have it whenever we fall short. We believe that anything less than perfection will be met with at least a good, sharp kick, or maybe even a serious disease, such as cancer.

The Bible tells us God is offended when we think of Him this way. Consider the parable of the talents. The unfaithful servant thought his master was "a hard man," so he hid the entrusted talent in the ground.[3] This made his master furious. How do *you* view God?

Since God is the source of all virtue, we can't experience one of His qualities while denying that He personifies that virtue. To get on the path of gentleness, then, we need to understand the depths of our Lord's gentleness.

THE GENTLE GOD

Though Jesus gave Himself a number of figurative titles (such as the Good Shepherd), when it came to actually describing His character with specific virtues, there are very few self-portraits. This gives any one description particular importance. When Jesus describes Himself in Matthew 11:28-30, gentleness tops the list: "I am gentle and humble in heart."

Before Jesus came, the prophets predicted that the Messiah would be known for His gentleness: "See, your king comes to you, gentle and riding on a donkey."[4] When the apostles looked back in memory of our Lord, they thought of this virtue: "By the meekness and gentleness of Christ, I appeal to you."[5]

The true Spirit of God is seen in another prophecy about the Messiah. Isaiah 42:3 foretold that the Christ would not break a "bruised reed" or snuff out a "smoldering wick." Even at its best, a reed is very weak, hollow, and fragile. A *bruised* reed depicts a spirit that is hanging on by a few threads. A smoldering wick depicts a spirit in which life and hope have all but vanished.

I've met many people like that, who feel as if one more shake will surely be their last and they'll fall apart. In businesses and churches, in stores and shopping malls, and even in ballparks, you'll see bruised reeds and smoldering wicks. Lonely, distant marriages; the ache of a child in rebellion; the seeming impossibility of ever making enough money to pay half the bills; the pervasive silence of God; the scars of past humiliation; two dozen people's worth of ailments in one body — the causes of bruised reeds are endless.

Do you ever feel as if you are "just making it?" If so, you may know the offensiveness of ungentle Christians who march onto the scene and make an already difficult situation intolerable. The guy who says, "Get over it." Or the woman who glibly comments: "Don't worry; Jesus took your baby to be with Him in heaven. You're young, you can have another." Or the legalist who charges "Obviously, you wouldn't sin if you loved the Lord. Are you sure you're saved?"

These people come with verbal saws to remove spiritual slivers. That's *not* an accurate depiction of Jesus. Jesus is the One who can touch you without breaking you. Jesus can gently nurse you back to spiritual health: "I am gentle and humble in heart and you will find rest for your souls."

The Spirit of the God-Man, who was sent to reveal the nature of our Creator, was clothed in gentleness; and this virtue allowed Him to enter into the lives of broken, hurting people. He wants to give us this same capacity for compassion.

THE GENTLE CHRISTIAN

The Bible is clear that those who call Christ their master will display the virtue of gentleness. Philippians 4:5 tells us, "Let your gentleness be evident to all." Colossians 3:12 adds, "Clothe yourselves with . . . gentleness." Paul is even more direct in 1 Timothy 6:11, telling us to "pursue" gentleness.

I've found that some of the most forceful men are often the most insecure. You'd think that if they could dish it out, they could take it, but that's rarely the case. My temptation is to respond in kind, but that serves only to perpetuate the disagreement. If I carefully measure my tone I can usually feel the tension dissipate between us.

Peter urged us to answer nonbelievers with "gentleness and respect." That means even the enemies of Christ, those who oppose Him and ridicule His followers, are to be treated with gentleness. In this, Peter suggests that gentleness is not a bonus we give to the deserving; it is a debt we owe to all.

Even fallen Christians can be won back by gentleness. Paul counsels in Galatians 6:1: "If someone is caught in a sin, you who are spiritual should restore him gently." Even though someone has brought shame on the name of Christ, we're urged to maintain a gentle spirit.

Paul even goes so far as to urge us to treat with gentleness those who oppose us, saying of Christian leaders, "Those who oppose him he must gently instruct."[6]

The legalist would protest, "They don't *deserve* to be treated respectfully," but this misses the point. The gospel isn't about winning an argument; it's about reconciling people to God and to each other. Brutish force doesn't reconcile, it divides; legalistic demands don't invite, they alienate. Grace and gentleness build bridges.

We can't shout people into righteousness. In fact, it has been my experience that those Christians who shout the loudest often have the most guilt-ridden consciences. What they need more than anything else is to be overwhelmed with the reality of the gentle God who loves them.

Since Paul urges Timothy to pursue gentleness, it must be possible to acquire this virtue in our own lives. Let's look at how that might take place.

BECOMING GENTLE PEOPLE

I was working on my car—always a frustrating experience for a mechanical klutz like me—and my youngest was keeping me company. As she inspected my tools, she opened my socket set. It was upside-down, so the sixty-four sockets rolled onto the sidewalk.

"Oh, Kelsey," I said. I didn't yell or even raise my voice. But she is so sensitive that just the tone was enough to elicit a pained expression. She started to walk toward the house, but I called after her.

"Kelsey!"

She turned.

"You didn't *mean* to do that. I'm not angry at you. It's all right."

Kelsey broke down, ran back to me, and buried her weeping face in my shoulder. Her actions reminded me of how easily people in this world are wounded. How delicate are the souls we encounter every day. We often miss this because, on the exterior, everybody looks fine, but inside, many are bruised reeds just waiting to topple over.

Why is it that "gentleness" makes us think "weakness" when gentleness gives incredible inner strength, self-control, and resilience? I was trying to sell a car one time, so I parked it in the outskirts of a shopping mall parking lot with a "For Sale" sign taped to the windows. Overnight, it was towed. I contacted the mall security, and they said they hadn't requested any towing, but I found out that a towing company had a contract. If they were experiencing a slow night, they could go "shopping" for cars to pick up.

It had been a stressful week, and I was already in a bad mood. And when I arrived at the towing office, things went from bad to worse. The personnel were abominable. The manager's wall was covered with photos of naked women. I was convinced this outfit was incapable of making an honest living as tow-truck operators and had instead become industrial vultures who preyed on honest people.

I lost my temper in their office. I let them know exactly what I thought. And I was wrong. My outburst of temper was a sign of *weakness*. Gentle strength — self-control with firmness — would have handled the difficult situation just as well, and done so in the spirit of Christ.

Gentleness is much more powerful than the human failings of temper, anger, and hatred. Anger has a place in the Christian life, as does confrontation. But gentleness will have a far bigger role to play than anger, for gentleness means understanding human frailty. It's a willingness to support, help, teach, and counsel with patience, until the other person becomes strong and mature. Gentleness also means the application of grace, and since grace is "unmerited favor," the true definition of gentleness is the application of unmerited favor.

This means no one has to earn my gentleness. Instead of hardening the manager with my anger, I could have brought the kindness of Christ to him.

How can we allow gentleness to cover us in such trying situations?

1. Remember the gentleness of Christ

The first step in becoming gentle is being overwhelmed by the gentleness with which God has treated us. I try to remind myself that I need to treat others like God has treated me. Gentleness doesn't call us to ignore people's failings—God doesn't ignore mine—but it does call me to respond in a particular way. The difference is really in methodology—*how* sin and weakness is confronted and handled, not whether it will be handled.

We are completely undeserving, dead in our sins, still failing on a daily basis, yet God doesn't write us off. He's still there, still forgiving, still loving, still nurturing. Accept this gentleness for yourself. If you find this to be a difficult exercise, use the spiritual discipline of scriptural meditation to shape your soul. Read slowly and thoughtfully over Matthew 21:5, 2 Corinthians 10:1, and Matthew 11:28-30. Let these passages feed your spirit and redirect your thinking so that you can understand the nature of the God who loves you.

2. Show gentleness to yourself

It is painful to hear people berating themselves for stupid things they did years ago. Maybe you did make a stupid business investment, but when did you expect to learn a lesson? Are we supposed to be born financially brilliant? Maybe you did fail sexually, but will you punish yourself for the rest of your life?

Sometimes people sin because they think they can fill a need . . . only to find that sin destroys and does not deliver what it promises. The spiritual life is one of learning and growing, and God, more than anyone else, understands this. Do we honestly think God expects us to go from eager pagan to Francis of Assisi in two weeks? This is not an apology for sin, but merely a plea for a realistic view of living.

Even though some of my actions have brought shame on the name of Christ, gentleness calls me to apply unmerited favor, based on the death and resurrection of Jesus.

3. Show gentleness to others

We can choose to live our life disappointed with everyone around us, or we can be armed with the virtue of gentleness and enter into the blessing of authentic relationship.

Let's remind ourselves of some spiritual truths: Nobody, apart from God, is perfect. Your spouse will fail you. Your children will disappoint you. Your pastor won't meet your expectations. The time will come, therefore, when you will have a legitimate gripe. You will be right, and they will be wrong. This is the crossroads of gentleness. Which path will you take? Condemnation and censure or the application of unmerited favor? Before you make that decision, remind yourself of how God has treated you.

Life is tough. It helps us to apply gentleness when we realize that people are being ground down all the time by the stuff of living. One time I took great offense when a woman I know snapped at me. I'd done nothing to provoke her. Later I learned that, due to financial difficulties, she and her husband had recently lost their home, and it looked as if they would lose their car.

No, it wasn't right for her to take her tension out on me, but I just happened to be there. As a Christian brother, I could absorb that frustration as a gift to her and to the gentle God who has treated me with unbelievable grace.

When a child comes home from school, seemingly bent on being deliberately difficult; when a spouse comes home from work and is being unfairly short-tempered; when a coworker snaps, I pause, pray, and consider: "What is this all about? What is really going on here?" And then, with self-control and grace, I can respond gently.

We can force people to do many things. And in forcing, we can break their spirit a little more or even drive them away from us altogether. The alternative is to draw them to us in the spirit of Christ; by the virtue of gentleness, to open their hearts to correction, learning, and growth. Perhaps most important, they can experience Christ in us.

Gentle living is blessed living. It's soothing, refreshing, bathing people in the presence of Christ. No wonder Edwards calls it "the Christian spirit." What else more accurately paints a picture of our Lord? What other virtue so radically gives us our life back from the frivolous judgments and misdirected angers of the world?

CHAPTER SIXTEEN

COURAGEOUS LIVING
(FORTITUDE)

Submitting to a tyrant is exactly the opposite of
submitting to a lover.
The first takes a diminution of spiritual energy,
the second takes an excess.

PETER KREEFT

IT WAS A DEATH SENTENCE, PURE AND SIMPLE. THE ONLY THING left, it seemed, was the dying.

Robert Kotlowitz had been assigned to the third platoon just minutes before, and now the master sergeant of C Company assigned Kotlowitz and two comrades to man the squad's Browning Automatic Rifle (BAR) unit.

Back at Fort Benning, Kotlowitz had learned a startling military fact—the life expectancy of the BAR team in combat was *eleven seconds*. "No, we were not thrilled," he admits, but there was nothing he could do. With what seems to me incredible courage, Kotlowitz accepted the challenge and survived the war.[1]

I was born in 1961, much too late to join Kotlowitz in World War II, yet I often wonder—how would I have done? But this question ignores the present spiritual challenge. Just as courage is highly valued in war, there is a comparable spiritual virtue that is essential for living the Christian faith, one that the ancients knew as *fortitude*—inner strength and spiritual courage.

DO NOT BE AFRAID

If you pick up a Bible concordance and look up the word "afraid," you'll notice how often these three words appear in front of it: "Do not be. . . ."

God tells Abram, "Do not be afraid."[2] He meets Abraham's son Isaac and tells him the same thing: "Do not be afraid."[3] Even after witnessing numerous victories and soul-stirring miracles, Moses had to be reminded, "Do not be afraid."[4]

In one of the more famous passages of the Bible, God tells Joshua to "be strong and of good courage; do not be afraid."[5] This is a particularly appropriate passage for us to look at, in that Israel's initial fear kept an entire generation out of the Promised Land. And because of their fear—this is important—they missed God's best.

Virtually every time God calls someone to do something in Scripture, He pleads with them, "Do not be afraid." "Joseph, do not be afraid to take Mary home as your wife."[6] "Paul, don't be afraid to keep preaching."[7] In Jesus' teaching and conversation, it seems like He spends half His words telling people not to fear.

Why all this attention? Perhaps it's because cowardice is one of the great life-thieves of all time. Shakespeare wrote, "Cowards die many times before their deaths, the valiant never taste of death but once."[8] Spiritual cowardice worms its way into our souls when our eyes become obsessively focused on our circumstances and we lose our interior vision of God as our soul's strength. Let's look at some of the immediate sources of cowardice and fear.

The first fear is the fear of *loss*. This is really the fear of being an orphan, as if we didn't have a heavenly Father to look after us. Since God is our benevolent provider, what could we possibly lose that He won't replace, if it's really necessary? If you sense this fear in your heart, ask yourself, *What do I really fear losing?* Then ask yourself, *Can't God provide what I really need?*

The second source of spiritual cowardice is *pride*, mixed with the fear of failure.

I remember hearing Billy Graham talk sheepishly about his first preaching experience, in which he had prepared two sermons for two nights and ended up preaching both of them the first night—and still ran out of material in ten minutes! What if, after that first experience,

Graham had let pride conquer his courage and he had insisted, "I'll never preach again?" Many choose safe lives in which failure (and therefore, real success) is highly unlikely. These people never take risks and they never fail, but they also die without any real service. They may never make a mistake, but they'll also never make a difference.

Jamie Buckingham, an insightful Christian writer and pastor, once recounted his experience when he performed baptisms at a packed-out Easter service. One of the people he baptized was unusually large, and the water level was raised to such a height that it flooded his waders, making it impossible for Jamie to get out. He had to climb out of those waders in his underwear, in full view of a laughing, full-capacity crowd.

If we want to serve God but demand that we never be embarrassed in the process, we're just giving in to spiritual cowardice and pride. We will make mistakes. We may even be humiliated. But there's a source of strength to see us through—the virtue of fortitude.

Another source of cowardice is *despair*. Sometimes we look at where we are and where we want to be, and the gulf seems so great that we think, "A million years will pass before I'll get anywhere near where I need to be; if I'm that far away, why try?"

Glory shines in the Christian who refuses to give up. She's beaten, she falls, she stumbles, she cracks, she breaks, she bends, but through it all, she keeps getting up. Sometimes, we can only grasp what is offered to us, and the courage not to quit is often the thread by which we maintain our Christian growth.

Yet a third cause of fear is the *heat of opposition*. We do not live in a world that is friendly to the God we serve. As Kreeft points out, "There are segments of the world where you can find acceptance even if you are a pervert, a punk, a sadist, or a snob. . . . [But] Christ and his Church are alien and threatening."[9]

If you're overly timid, easily cowed, and afraid to speak up, you will find it extremely difficult, perhaps even impossible, to walk in the character of Christ. When I read about Jesus standing up among the Sanhedrin, boldly facing His enemies and courageously speaking the truth, I marvel at His fortitude. He knew the plots that were being hatched in their hearts. He knew these people would put Him to death. But He spoke the truth all the same.

What is the foundation of this essential virtue of Christ?

THE NATURE OF FORTITUDE

Fortitude is more than forcing yourself to put on a brave face. A soldier making a seemingly courageous charge in battle could be acting out of sheer cowardice. Maybe he fears his fellow soldiers' taunts more than he fears bullets. He could be running *from* ridicule even more than he is running *toward* the enemy.

Fortitude is an inner strength that relies on the provision of God to help both our minds and our hearts to respond in a Christ-like manner. Edwards points out, "many people seem to be quite mistaken concerning the nature of Christian fortitude. It is quite the opposite of brutal fierceness such as the boldness of beasts of prey. Rather, true Christian fortitude consists of a strength of mind, through grace. . . . It overrules and suppresses evil, unruly passions and affections of the mind. And it exerts steadfastly and freely good affections and dispositions without being hampered by sinful fear or the opposition of enemies."[10]

Christ's fortitude provides an internal power that gives us the strength to pursue a course that frightens the natural man inside us. For example, it is demonstrated by a dissatisfied wife who walks away from an affair which promises emotional satisfaction but spiritual devastation. Urgent longings in her heart tell her to abandon her vows but, through fortitude, she has the courage to walk away from that affair, and trust God to meet her needs — even though she knows she is returning to a distant marriage and an inattentive husband.

Fortitude gives us the strength to live in a world of cancer, disaster, atrocities, temptation, betrayal, and hardship, all the while maintaining a calm, steadfast spirit. One Christian might hear the words, "the tumor is malignant" and immediately his faith shatters and breaks. A Christian armed with fortitude will know that God can work even through this. Even though the immediate future seems bleak, he chooses to trust in the ultimate goodness of God.

Have you ever experienced this inner strength and control? Have you been led by what is right, true, holy, and good — even when you felt afraid, tempted, angry, and bitter? How can we begin to practice fortitude in our own lives?

Toward Fortitude

Bellingham, Washington, is a relatively safe community. But shortly after moving back here, my family faced some insidious predators. These visitors came at night, and they helped themselves to our food. They didn't take any money, but they left enough evidence of their foraging that my wife refused to go downstairs in the morning until I went there first and checked everything out.

Finally, one fateful evening, I came face to face with one of them. A good friend of mine, Rob, had just come over. When I stood up and turned to go downstairs to greet Rob, I saw one of these intruders coldly staring at me, just a foot or so from the desk where I had been working. I chased the unwelcome visitor into my son's room and shouted to Rob.

"Come up here and help me catch this mouse!"

The thing that amazed me was that I was feeling a little jittery. I'm nearly six feet tall, and this furry little thing could fit inside a hamburger bun; even so, neither Rob nor I wanted to get all that close to it.

How could something as small and harmless as a mouse cause so much fear? *All* our fears would have this same lack of rationality if we took the time to dissect them. Ungodly fear—from a Christian per-spective—comes from forgetting basic spiritual truths. The first step toward fortitude is dissecting our fears to find out what it really is that we're afraid of, then asking ourselves, is this fear legitimate?

When we take the time to look at our fears in this way, most often we'll find that the fear overlooks God's active presence. If the fear is one of loss, remind yourself of God's promised provision. If the fear is one of ridicule, thank God you have an opportunity to grow in humility! Remind yourself that nothing can happen to you apart from God's watchful care. He doesn't blink, and He can use any circum-stance for His good purpose.

Just as discernment springs from meditating on the beauty of God, so fortitude is born when we meditate on the greatness of God. From the psalms of Moses and David, we read about men making God the soul's fortress, shield, hiding place, dwelling place, high tower, and high rock. Because these men had made God their soul's *internal* fortress, they could take *external* risks. By meditating on the greatness of God, they feared losing their grip on God's presence more than they feared losing their physical lives. This is basic Christianity. Jesus taught us, "Do not be afraid of those who kill the body and after that can do no more. But I will show you whom you should fear: Fear him who, after the killing of the body, has power to throw you into hell. Yes, I tell you, fear him."[11]

When we are lost in the greatness of God, we realize that there is no physical, emotional, or social loss so great that God cannot bring good out of it and compensate us in the next life. Psalms 47, 48, 99, 111, and 145 are excellent psalms to pray over or commit to memory.

Franklin Graham, president of Samaritan's Purse, is someone who models Christian fortitude. I've asked him, "Why are you so willing to risk your life by going into areas in the midst of a raging civil war?"

Franklin responded, "First, I don't risk my life foolishly. But second, if God has called me to be there, who am I to question Him?" And listen to Franklin's conclusion: "Besides, what is the worst thing that could happen to me? If I was seriously injured, I could still serve God — just look at the life of Joni Eareckson Tada, for instance.[12] And if I died, that instant I'd be in heaven with Jesus."

Franklin's boldness has come from comparing the earthly consequences of his obedience to God with the eternal blessings that will follow.

The perspective that has helped lodge fortitude in my soul comes from the psalmist: "The LORD is my light and my salvation — whom shall I fear? The LORD is the stronghold of my life — of whom shall I be afraid?" (Psalm 27:1).

For me, gaining fortitude was virtually synonymous with gaining a God-centered orientation. When I rely on my own strength alone, I put myself at the center of the universe — *I* have to provide for my family, *I* have to make things happen in the church, *I* have to take care of myself. When I take on Christ's attitude of full trust in God, I learn to rest in His provision, purpose, and benevolence.

We need to learn to leave the outcome of our battles to the Lord. It is when we try to control outcomes that we fail to have real faith in Him. The fortitude of Christ gives us a supreme calmness, the ability to calculate in peace rather than frenzy, and the courage to take the steps we need to take to act as people of faith.

A good friend of mine was agonizing over whether to start a new church. He believed God had called him; other pastors confirmed that calling; he had displayed the giftings of a pastor, but what about the financial needs of his family? What about the possibility that the new church might fail? What about a possible adverse reaction from surrounding churches and Christians?

More good works of God have probably been destroyed by the fear mongering "what ifs" than by Satan. If everybody who does anything for God had to have $100,000 in savings and the unanimous approval of those around them, *nothing would ever get started.* Serving God entails risk. There are no guarantees we will not fail — but the unwillingness to risk may be our greatest failure of all.

And after we step out, fortitude will be even more important. Recently, I was in a situation where, though I had done my best to follow God in my life, it seemed the whole world was caving in on me. I remember dropping to my knees and calling out to God for the strength and direction just to get through the day. All my problems and challenges couldn't possibly be solved in twenty-four hours. Fortitude, for me, simply meant the willingness to keep moving forward — being a faithful steward of the here and now, and not growing faint of heart. God didn't whisper, "Everything will be fine in another month or so." He just led me to not give up and to leave the results to Him.

INTIMATE CHALLENGE

An elderly man shuffled through the Smithsonian museum in Washington, D.C. Since he was wearing a disguise, no one recognized him. As a young man, his celebrity had cost him dearly. Not only had he forfeited all sense of privacy, but fame had ultimately resulted in the tragic kidnapping and death of his son. He was not here to be fawned over; he simply wanted to spend time with an old friend.

He went straight to the exhibit he had come to see and there, suspended from the ceiling, was his cherished partner-in-adventure: the *Spirit of St. Louis.*

Charles Lindbergh looked at his famous airplane and smiled. Many men had died trying to do what he and this collection of bolts and metal had accomplished — the amazing, first transatlantic flight, a difficult and dangerous feat in those first days of aviation.

There were so many ways that Lindbergh's flight could have killed him, it's a wonder he had the courage to leave the ground. The flight took over thirty hours, and he'd gotten no sleep the night before takeoff. In fact, disaster nearly struck within seconds of Lindbergh leaving the ground. The airfield was muddy, and the *St. Louis* was so heavy with fuel that people drew in their breath as his plane narrowly missed nearby power lines.

But Lindbergh faced those fears, and in that process his heart was wedded to a machine which he regularly visited in his old age.

Few things will build intimacy with God as much as facing your fears with Him. Just as Lindbergh's soul was knit to a plane, so will ours be knit to God when we learn to trust in Him alone, obeying His will even when we are afraid. After God leads me through a seemingly perilous situation, I'm all His. It's the most glorious, intimate fulfillment I've ever known.

Don't run from your fears. Walk straight through them. Armed with the virtue of fortitude, you will enter into the very center of God's heart.

CHAPTER SEVENTEEN

ENLARGED LIVING
(OBEDIENCE)

The gospel keeps many a one from the jail and gallows,
even if it does not keep him from hell.
GEORGE WHITEFIELD

Men question the truth of Christianity
because they hate the practice of it.
ROBERT SOUTH

—◄O►—

P ASTOR MIKE FEHLAUER SAT IN HIS CAR AS HIS CONGREGATION filed into the church building. Though he had started the church with just a few couples, it had grown to over four hundred individuals. Mike appeared to be a very successful pastor.

While clergy typically pray before a church service, on this day Mike fingered the gun that lay beside him, a loan from a church member for "target practice." He finally picked the gun up, and slowly slid the barrel into his mouth.

Mike felt what he calls a "demonic rush" to pull the trigger, almost a thrill at the very thought of it.

Inside his church, a woman was overwhelmed by a sense that she needed to pray and plead for her pastor's life. She didn't know why, but she prayed with everything she had.

Back out in the car, Mike felt as if he'd been shaken awake. *What are you doing?* he thought. The gun came out.

What was going on? For years, Pastor Fehlauer had been caught in the crush of a secret battle with lust. His church continued to grow, his sexual relationship with his wife appeared healthy, but every few months, Mike would cave in. His addiction started out with pornography, graduated to the world of strip clubs, and eventually led Mike to visit prostitutes. The tension created by his secret life of disobedience led him to want to kill himself.

Disobedience doesn't always lead us to such desperation, of course. Sometimes, it simply evokes a weariness with Christianity, a sense of disconnectedness, or a quiet despair.

Obedience gives us our life back by creating desires that Jesus promises can be met: "Blessed are those who hunger and thirst for righteousness, *for they will be filled*."[1]

This "filling" is what we truly crave because God created us to crave it. Obedience is really the desire to live deeply, thoughtfully, and in communion with God in the everyday pathways of our lives. It's the only life that brings true, lasting fulfillment and the inner satisfaction of being filled.

THE TRUTH OF OUR HEART

In 1991, a widow in Maryland filed a tax return for her deceased husband. Imagine her surprise when the IRS responded with a letter addressed to *her spouse*: "We are processing your gift tax return for calendar year 1990 and find we need more information. Please provide your date of death. . . . Thank you for your cooperation."[2]

For all of us, it's not the IRS we'll need to be concerned with after our death, it's the judgment seat of God. And one thing you notice immediately about Jesus' judgment-seat teachings is the surprise of those being judged.[3]

Some people, Jesus tells us, think they're doing fine with God. They don't have a care in the world about their spiritual condition, yet they are living on the precipice of an eternity in hell.

How can this be?

The Bible is explicitly clear about the human heart; it is deceitful above all things.[4] Paul added that just because his conscience is clear doesn't mean he is, in fact, innocent.[5] Yet *feeling*—that pillar of modern religion—continues to be the guide of many Christians: As long as we feel okay, we assume we must *be* okay. Since we don't experience any pervasive guilt, we must be generally on track with God. But in Matthew 25, when Jesus talked about the judgment, He didn't point to feelings, He pointed to actions.

While the essence of transformation is a regeneration of our souls from within, it is heresy to then suggest that actions don't matter. Obedience matters very much. As Jonathan Edwards points out, "The Scripture plainly teaches that practice is the best evidence of the sincerity of Christians. Our reason teaches the same thing."[6]

In this regard, New Agers have it easy — all those adherents need is to be sincere and tolerant. As long as they occasionally engage in some study or spiritual ritual that gives them an inner thrill, they can call themselves "spiritual" people — regardless of whether their hearts are changing, transforming the way they treat other people.

In contrast, Edwards writes that "Christian practice is much more to be preferred as evidence of salvation than sudden conversion, mystical enlightenment, or the mere experience of emotional comfort."[7]

If only we could prove the sincerity of our faith by the spiritual raptures we experience during worship, the sudden sparks of insight that clearly come from God, or the depth of our feeling following conversion! But the shallowness of this is readily apparent. I can give my wife Valentine, anniversary, and birthday cards like clockwork. I can say all the right words. But if I keep a mistress on the side, will anybody suggest that I truly love my wife? Or will it matter at all that I wept with joy on our wedding day if, ten years later, I'm a chronically selfish and critical husband?

Edwards points us to the bare essentials: "The proper test of what man really prefers is to see what he actually cleaves to and practices when given a choice. . . . [G]odliness consists not merely in having a heart intent on doing the will of God, *but having a heart that actually does it.* . . . It is absurd then to pretend to have a good heart while living a wicked life."[8]

Or a halfhearted one.

When we face temptation and the core of our will is exposed, we must ask ourselves, *Do I love God, or not?* Jesus was refreshingly blunt: "If you love me, you will obey what I command."[9]

I tend to make "excuses" for my self-indulgence: "I was tired, I've been really stressed. If I had been in my right mind, and at full strength, I wouldn't have fallen." This kind of cover-up talk will not even get you by a good therapist, let alone God. The truth is not just that temptation hits us *when* we're weak, but that it also assaults us *where* we're weak.

Edwards again: "If we want to know whether a building will stand strong or not, we look at it *when the wind is blowing hard.* Similarly, we can list the reality of a man's Christian practice when he is under the trials of God's providence."[10]

The best thing we can do for ourselves is to regularly strip away all our excuses and ask how we are doing in regard to obedience. Don't fool yourself. Don't play games. Be honest with yourself and with God. How are you doing, really, in terms of actual obedience?

SHRUNKEN LIVING

I've spoken with Mike Fehlauer on the phone. God has restored him and given him a greater ministry now that he has faced the truth in himself. He often travels around the country, sometimes with his wife, giving his testimony. But there are some things he simply can't do. He can't be alone on the road, for instance, for any length of time. A local pastor knows where he is at virtually all times. Even something inno-cent—like a painting or a sculpture in a museum—can stir up tremendous urges if the wrong image presents itself to Mike's eye. His past disobedience has left a mark: It has shrunken Mike's world, and he knows he is safer living within tighter boundaries as he re-learns healthy heart attitudes toward women and sexuality.

Sin, while promising to enlarge our experience, actually ends up limiting it. Someone who has never struggled with alcohol abuse can walk into a restaurant that serves alcohol and be completely relaxed. A recovering alcoholic knows better than to try this too soon after sobering up.

If sin limits our lives in this way, where is its draw? The draw to sin comes from the fact that we are spiritually hungry people who want to be, in Jesus' words, filled. Sin provides a temporary break from reality—a momentary hit that removes the pain of separation from God. But here's the tragedy: It ultimately pushes us further from God, causing our spiritual emptiness to grow over the long run. God made us in such a way that *only* those who search after righteousness will be filled. We can't be filled by sin—but we often think we can.

Another cause of disobedience is flat-out rebellion. Some of us just don't care about God's prior claim on our lives. We want salvation—and then we want to live a life of total autonomy from God, without responsibility, wallowing in selfish indulgence.

This attitude opens the door to full-blown spiritual idolatry—but I'm not talking about bowing down to statues. When worship is looked at in terms of my devotion, expenditure of time, energy, talents, and money, then the reality of what's going on inside my heart becomes much clearer.

You and I spend our strength and resources serving *something*. What is it? A hobby? Happiness? A secret sin? A certain lifestyle? Gaining the respect of others? Security?

If the primary pursuit of your heart is anything other than learning to cooperate with God in the outworking of your life, you will always lack fullness within and eventually will find yourself in desperate spiritual straits.

We need to understand the cyclical nature of the spiritual life. Just as gravity pulls all things down physically, so sin pulls all things down spiritually. We are spiritual beings, and one of the truths resulting from that is that sin gives birth to increased temptation. The more you sin, the harder it becomes to stop sinning. If you stay away from that sin for awhile, it will be easier to avoid it the next time.

The Bible warns us that gradual degeneration is the normal course of sin. Consider the experience of Hazael, who was confronted by Elisha with all the wicked things he would do one day: "You will set fire to [the Israelites'] fortified places, kill their young men with the sword, dash their little children to the ground, and rip open their pregnant women."[11] Hazael is horrified and disbelieving: "How could I, a mere dog, accomplish such a feat?" he asks. In his worst nightmares, Hazael can't imagine himself ripping open pregnant women. Yet the very next day, Hazael murders Ben-Hadad by suffocating him with a thick cloth, beginning his ugly reign by killing another man.

Notice this: Hazael didn't start out with mass murder. He began his wicked career with a solitary act of homicide. He *waded* into sin, as all of us do, and once it got hold of him, he could do things that would have made him retch in a previous season.

Prisons are filled with men and women who thought they'd "borrow" a little money from their company but ended up becoming out-and-out embezzlers.

J. C. Ryle points out, "There are two ways of going to hell; one is to walk into it with your eyes open—few people do that; the other is to go down by the steps of little sins—and that way, I fear, is only too common."[12]

If we enter the slope of sin, there is no guarantee that we can stop at our chosen progression: "I'll go this far, and then stop." It is a major presumption to assume that you can plateau at any one level.

If you truly want God to give you your life back, you must begin to pay attention to the "Do Not Enter" signs posted in front of certain behaviors, thought patterns, and attitudes.

The virtue of obedience is your guardian and your protector to keep you from hurting yourself as well as others, not to mention to prevent you from offending your God.

How do we practice this attitude of Christ?

THE POWER OF OBEDIENCE

Reebok™ pays Henry "Que" Gaskins almost $100,000 a year to keep professional basketball player Allen Iverson on the straight and narrow. Gaskins is part of a growing cadre of assigned mentors hired by athletic shoe manufacturers to keep endorsement athletes out of trouble.[13] Why would Reebok™ pay someone a six-figure income to look after an athlete? They're protecting their investment. Reebok™ has a $40 million contract with Iverson, so spending $100,000 to keep him out of trouble is a relatively small insurance premium.

You and I do not have companies paying someone a large salary to keep us on the path of obedience, but we do have the Holy Spirit, who works within us to woo and inspire us toward holiness. And so, for us, the path to obedience is a path that begins in the interior life.

We start by confronting the two primary causes of sin: pain and rebellion. In a moment of prayer, submit both to God. Pay particular attention to releasing the interior demands that insist your perceived needs give you the right to go hunting for satisfaction.

It's easier to align our actions with God's will when our *heart* is set on pleasing God. We should work toward the ideal of the psalmist who said he "delights" in God's law.[14] Ryle points out that Paul told the Romans to abhor what is evil.[15]

If we court and tease and promote temptation, we're calling into question the integrity of our faith. As Ryle explains, "What is the use of your praying, 'Lead us not into temptation,' unless you are yourself careful not to run into it; and 'deliver us from evil,' unless you show a desire to keep out of its way?"[16]

I stress this interior step first because that's what gives us the power to embark on the second step: taking little steps of obedience. Let interior obedience begin building in your heart until it brings you to an external victory. One act of obedience builds momentum toward a fully virtuous life. John of the Cross explains, "An act of virtue produces in the soul mildness, peace, comfort, light, purity, and strength, just as an inordinate appetite brings about torment, fatigue, weariness, blindness, and weakness. Through the practice of one virtue all the virtues grow, and similarly, through an increase of one vice, all the vices and their effects grow."[17]

Obedience is life giving. It strengthens us and renews our spirits in a quiet and steady way. Just try it and see!

Disobedience, in contrast, eventually saps our energy, gives birth to listlessness and discouragement, and often takes us right down to despair.

Which life do you want to pursue?

The most decisive step toward obedience is to renounce self-centered living. At its root, sin is self-obsession. A mother lashing out in anger at her children is thinking about *her* frustration, not the effect her words will have on them. If you are struggling mightily against a sin, examine your heart's attitude; isn't there a selfish demand and focus buried deep within?

How do we confront this obsession with ourselves? By moving beyond merely avoiding evil, and focusing on working *toward* the higher calling God has placed on our lives—a life of service and mission.

Edwards connects the growth and integrity of our faith with our growth in the attitude of Christ: that we are here in service to God. From this perspective, sin is just one of many things that keeps us from becoming the man or woman God created us to be. Trials (things that make our life difficult), lusts and corruptions (things that tempt us and draw us away from our purpose), and sufferings (things that would steal our attention from others and cause us to focus on ourselves) will all assault us. But the attitude of a servant will empower you to push through and complete your mission before God.

OBEDIENCE AND THE LONG ROAD

Real obedience is cultivated and demonstrated over years and decades. Its genuineness is proven when obedience gets truly hard—when it makes no sense, but you pursue God nonetheless.

I know a part-time, middle-aged pastor whose primary business has been slowly declining for many years as he works to support himself in ministry. It would be so easy for him to drop his calling as a pastor and focus full-time on his business. He has lived with this tension for a number of years, and nobody could accuse him of not trying hard enough. What impresses me about him is that he isn't demanding release. He is pursuing the long road of obedience. Where does he find the staying power?

It comes from the fact that he is motivated by the mission God has given him. This fuels his obedience, even in difficult circumstances.

Obedience is our calling, our cover, our privilege, and our honor, precisely because of *Who* we're called to be obedient *to*. Obedience to God means freedom from the crowd's opinion, deliverance from our own rank desires, and liberation from the tyranny and stranglehold of sin. Obedience is the spiritual attitude of Christ that completes the clothing of ourselves in His character.

There's a world of difference between Jesus in Gethsemane, courageously and obediently agreeing to lay down His life according to God's will, and a pastor sticking a gun in his mouth according to his despair. Which life will you choose?

Obedience, ironic as it seems, will give you back the life you want to live, a life of fullness, mission, and purpose.

CHAPTER EIGHTEEN

THE RENEWAL OF FAITH
(PENITENCE)

When we die, we will not be criticized for having failed to work miracles. We will not be accused of having failed to be theologians or contemplatives. But we will certainly have some explanation to offer to God for not having mourned unceasingly.

JOHN CLIMACUS

God, in hating our sin,
is like a surgeon who hates the cancer
only because he loves the patient.

PETER KREEFT

AFTER FOUR HUNDRED YEARS — ALMOST TWICE AS LONG AS THE United States has been a sovereign nation — finally, someone sent from God had begun to speak. The time between the Testaments — from the last words captured in the Old Testament to the first words uttered in the New Testament — was an excruciatingly silent four centuries.

To give you an idea how long four hundred years is, four centuries ago Shakespeare's Globe Theater was just opening and his play, *Much Ado About Nothing,* was showing to its first audience. Galileo was finishing his draftsman's compass, and John Calvin was dead, but only for about thirty years. Jamestown, the first European colony on the North American continent, was still a decade away from being formed.

Four hundred years is a long time, but that's how long it had been since God had spoken to His people Israel. And now, out in the desert, that silence was at last being broken. A forceful and simple man named John drew people who were famished for God's Word.

When you haven't spoken to someone in four hundred years, you choose your first words carefully. This is not the time to deal with peripheral matters. This is the time to get at root issues. After all, these words would re-establish history's most important love affair between a people and their God.

Does it surprise you, then, that the very first word God used to re-establish His relationship with the nation of Israel was "repent"?[1]

Within months after uttering this word so forcefully, John the Baptist was slammed into prison. Apparently, his teaching wasn't so popular. But John had testified that he was just a messenger, one sent to point the way to an even more important voice, that of the Messiah. What would *He* say? Would He contradict John, maybe put a little softer edge on God's message? There must have been tremendous excitement in the heavenlies as the angels bent their ears to hear the message that God so desperately wanted His people to hear, a message so important that the Son humbled Himself, took on the nature of flesh, and submitted to an arduous life on the planet called earth just to bring it to some fallen humans.

And then, Jesus spoke the same words uttered by John: "Repent, for the kingdom of heaven is near."[2]

The Christian's spiritual life doesn't begin with hope. It doesn't begin with chastity. It doesn't even begin with obedience. It begins, according to the book of Matthew, with penitence.

Penitence is being willing to exchange my old view of the things that I think will give me inner life for the things from God that really will give life and health. It involves sorrow for going the wrong way and a willingness to turn toward the right way. It's a change of heart accompanied by a change of mind, perfected by a change of direction — all three changes bending toward the will of God.

Since penitence is the spiritual counterbalance that rights us after our failure to obey God, it is the virtue that keeps us connected to the life-giving fellowship of God. Penitence returns us to humble reliance as it releases in us a spirit of surrender.

A DEATH SENTENCE

There's a startling passage in the book of Ezekiel. God calls six men to face Jerusalem, battle axes in hand. One of the men has a writer's inkhorn at his side, and God addresses him first: "Go through the midst of Jerusalem, and put a mark on the foreheads of the men who sigh and cry over all the abominations that are done within it." Then, to the others, God says, "Go after him through the city and kill; do not let your eye spare, nor have pity . . . but do not come near anyone on whom is the mark; and begin at My sanctuary."[3]

It's sobering, but true: The people who lack penitence are given the death sentence; the people who mourn are saved. Those who lived in a corrupt culture without any sense of grief and anguish were considered by God as unfit to live. There's something about penitence that softens God's heart and opens His favor.

In fact, the first two beatitudes in Jesus' famous Sermon on the Mount are related to penitence: "Blessed are the poor in spirit, for theirs is the kingdom of heaven. Blessed are those who mourn, for they will be comforted."[4] Not only was penitence God's first Word to His people, it provided the entry point for Jesus' first major address in the New Testament.

But why is penitence so crucial? One of the reasons God views our turning from sin with such tender affection is that sin itself is so deadly.

A DANGEROUS GAME

I had a crazy dream once, but in this case, the analogy fit the lesson. In my dream, I had offended the mob. They sent a "strong man" to straighten me out. He was polite to my family, friendly to my wife and kids, and acted like his only purpose was to be the kind counselor who would set me back on the right path.

We discussed what I had done, and I took the liberty of explaining my fault. The mob man smiled, nodded, added a correction or two, and then we began to part. Because he acted like a kindly uncle, I assumed all was going to be okay, so just as my family got out of hearing range, I asked him, "But what is to happen to me?"

"Oh, I'm going to have to kill you," he said. "There's no doubt about that. Nothing personal, though. I actually really like you."

When I awoke, I realized that sin is just like the Mafia. It pretends to be your friend, but it's a liar. Are you lonely? Sin has an answer. Frustrated? Sin has a delicious solution. Bored? Sin has a "cure."

And so we taste—just a little. We make friends with sin, never intending to sign up for full-fledged membership. But what makes us think we can do business with the mob—or evil—and get away unburned? The mob is, after all, the mob. And sin is, after all, sin. Satan comes only to steal, kill, and destroy.[5] If we live in Satan's world, we'll be robbed, killed, and ruined.

You can rationalize sin; you can flirt with it, but remember who and what you're flirting with. Sin is a date from hell, and however much hell acts like your friend, hell hates you with a passion that is terrifying in its intensity: *Oh, I'm going to have to kill you. Nothing personal, though.* Kreeft puts it this way: "The smallest sin is a small spark from the one fire that is Hell-fire."[6]

Sin burns us up. The tragedy is that some of us seem determined to burn as much as possible without being consumed. We hope to escape just barely having tasted as much sin (and therefore hell) as possible while still slipping into heaven.

This is a radically dangerous game. Our capacity to endure sin is unknown. "No one knows how long a human soul can endure the flames of sin before it dies."[7] If we visit hell, we may find that the doors have locked behind us before we realized visiting hours were over.

Do you really want to play that game?

The great value of penitence is that it keeps us out of the path of our soul's enemy, who wants to kill us. It directs us back into the path of God, in the obedient attitude of Jesus, who has come to give us life.

How do we grow in the heart and practice of penitence?

THE PATH OF PENITENCE

In 1990, Wham-O, the company that makes Frisbees, shipped 7,000 plastic disks to a nun who works at an Angolan orphanage. The chairman of the company, John Bowes, received the following reply: "The dishes you sent are wonderful. We eat all our meals off them. And the most amazing thing has happened. Some of the children are throwing them as sort of a game. This may be an idea for you."[8]

Frisbees can double as dishes, but they were made to be something else. Using them as plates is a devaluation of sorts — any flat object can hold food, but not every round object can fly so far and so well.

Likewise, we can devalue our lives with artificially busy pursuits. Humans can spend seventy years living for the next paycheck, the next sexual experience, the next vacation . . . or the next chance to cheat someone. But we were made to fly in God's will, and that's where we'll find the glory of virtuous life on earth.

The first step toward penitence comes from wanting to experience the full design of God's life for us. It is not fueled by morbid sorrow for our sins, but by the joy of *becoming*. God made us to become like Christ as we work to advance His kingdom on this earth. Any other end is a sad misuse of the eight or nine decades God gives us. This is the change of heart that makes up the basis of penitence — a desire to be properly aligned with God, to fulfill all His goals for us.

Second, we need to grieve over the lost years of our sin. We need to mourn the wasted hours, energy, and resources. This often involves simply taking the time to prayerfully and honestly examine what our sin has cost us and others — including how it offends God.

Painful as it is, do not be afraid to let anguish wash over you. Eventually, it will wash through you and leave you ready to begin again. If you haven't been taught to mourn, meditatively read through the book of Lamentations and the first chapter of Joel. It's helpful to use Scripture to guide our prayers in this, as the Bible reminds us that healthy remorse doesn't lead to despair. For example, Joel promises: "Turn to me with all your heart, with fasting, with weeping, and with mourning. So rend your heart, and not your garments; return to the LORD your God, for He is gracious and merciful, slow to anger, and of great kindness; and He relents from doing harm."[9]

True penitence will lead you from expressing your sorrow to God to expressing your sorrow to others. You may well need to ask forgiveness from those against whom you've sinned. Unresolved sin is a weight, and unreconciled relationships are a tether. If we want to fly high, we need to fly free.

The final step toward penitence is using God's design on our lives to inform our future choices. When we realize we were made to fly, we won't settle for less. Why give our bodies to sin when God has made them temples of His Holy Spirit?

Let's use the virtue of penitence to turn from those things that hold us back, to grieve over the lost years, and to be set free to make the best use of whatever time we have left. Let's also remember the many other benefits of penitence.

THE BENEFITS OF PENITENCE

You can spot a person who is a stranger to penitence with relative ease: Simply look for someone who is dominated and controlled by anger. The ancients teach that penitence breaks the ungodly human anger that rules our hearts. The penitent "no longer [knows] what it [is] for a man to be angry, for grief [has] done away with [his] capacity for rage."[10] Later, Climacus adds, "The tears of genuine mourning can extinguish every flame of anger and irascibility."[11]

Just as penitence draws us into God's presence, so anger pushes us away. Climacus explains, "If it is true that the Holy Spirit is peace of soul . . . then there is no greater obstacle to the presence of the Spirit in us than anger."[12]

The nature of anger is such that it hangs on to us with a ferocious tenacity. We think we've shaken it off, only to find it festering and growing stronger under the surface. While the object of our anger is often completely oblivious to our seething rage, we're poisoning our souls, pumping bucketfuls of spiritual bile into our system.

The longer we allow something to fester, the worse it grows. As an amateur student of history, I've read numerous books on famous wars. Many times, particularly in earlier wars, soldiers didn't die because of a bullet or a cannon shot. They died of an infection following the gunshot because sanitary medical assistance was miles away (or wasn't thought of yet). The same principle holds true spiritually. It may not be the initial sin that gets us, but the ensuing infection that seethes through our souls. Penitence breaks that process and cleans us out: "A fresh, warm wound is easier to heal than those that are old, neglected, and festering, and that need extensive treatment, surgery, bandaging, and cauterization. Long neglect can render many of them incurable."[13]

When we repent, it becomes much harder, spiritually, to judge others or to hold a grudge. When we experience God's rich forgiveness, it becomes much easier to offer that forgiveness, even to the undeserving.

Another great benefit of penitence is an ironic one. Surprisingly, penitence is the spiritual prelude to true celebration. People caught in the world are deadened by sin and are frequently numb to what is happening within them. Penitence sets us free to experience true contrition, but this is the gateway also to experience true joy. "The man who mourns constantly in a way that pleases God does not cease to celebrate daily. . . . The man wearing blessed, God-given mourning like a wedding garment gets to know the spiritual laughter of the soul."[14]

How we need this "laughter of the soul" which comes when I understand that God loves me anyway; though I left Him in my sin, He never left me and never stopped loving me. Climacus explains that "compunction is properly a gift from God, so that there is a real pleasure in the soul, since God secretly brings consolation to those who in their heart of hearts are repentant."[15]

This is a truth that Jesus Himself explained. Remember the second beatitude? Jesus promised that those who mourn will be comforted. What loving parent leaves a child in genuine mourning alone? The parent goes up to that child, puts an arm around her shoulder, and speaks tender words. Often, the parent will try to make the child laugh, just for good measure.

God is like that. Our mourning calls Him, and He rushes to guide us straight into the celebration of His heart.

Another benefit of penitence is that it keeps us in the childlike spirit so often praised by our Lord. This is a teaching that goes completely against modern, conventional wisdom: "Nearly all our modern psychologies tell us how to be 'adult,' 'mature,' and 'take-charge,' 'responsible for our own lives.' Kreeft writes, "when you see these ubiquitous code words . . . remember what they are: the old paganism in new dress. Remember what *adult* suggests in our culture. Remember what *adult* books, magazines, and movies are like. Remember that Jesus *never* told us to be 'adult' but instead said, 'Unless you . . . become as little children, you will by no means enter the Kingdom of Heaven' (Matthew 18:3). Heaven's gate is too tiny for any but a child. It is the eye of a needle. Large adult camels must go home to die or be born again as little children."[16]

Penitence reminds us that we are God's children. It is the gateway to the virtue of humility, which we explained earlier as the chief Christian virtue. It is impossible to be proud and penitent. If you have difficulty experiencing the virtue of humility, go through the "back door" of penitence.

But the last benefit of penitence we'll mention here may be the most important. I do not want to suggest that by "God giving us our lives back," the virtues point only to an earthly existence. In one sense, we've used this phrase figuratively, but in this sense, it once again becomes literal. Those who have never repented are doomed to eternal separation from God. Hell is real, an excruciating, disastrous, and eternal existence full of pain and futile longing.

Yet penitence, when it is offered through Jesus by faith, is accepted by God, who then applies the sacrifice of Jesus to wipe out a lifetime of sin, thereby sparing us from the horrible future we deserve. The thief on the cross had just one thing going for him, a penitent heart, and Jesus promised him that this was enough to enter paradise.[17] For all we know, that thief didn't tithe a single cent during his entire life. He didn't spend a single minute in an evangelical "quiet time" of devotion. He didn't go to synagogue or do good deeds or refrain from sin or sing any songs in worship. Religion and obedience did not save him. But because he spoke to the right Person, a single act of penitence wiped out the penalties justly accrued over the course of his entire life. He was like a worker hired at literally the last minute of the day who still received a full day's wages.

So, penitence renews our faith; breaks down our anger and our pride; leads us into true celebration; helps us maintain a childlike spirit; and ultimately leads us into our heavenly home. Because the virtues are something we practice imperfectly rather than own, penitence serves as the crucial connecting link to keep us on the path of growth. We will fail, but God has provided for that with a precious virtue called penitence.

Get your life back. Practice penitence.

AFTERWORD

And we, who with unveiled faces all reflect the Lord's glory, are
being transformed into his likeness with ever-increasing glory,
which comes from the Lord, who is the Spirit.
2 CORINTHIANS 3:18

HAVE YOU EVER NOTICED HOW COUPLES WHO HAVE BEEN MARRIED for a long time start to look alike? Twelve years ago, when a full-blooded Japanese friend of mine, Rob Takemura, married a fair-skinned redhead named Jill, we joked, "Yeah, now Rob and Jill will start to look alike."

This was said completely in jest; it was difficult to imagine how a Japanese man could ever look like a red-headed woman. Rob and Jill remain my wife's and my closest friends, but during the stretch that we lived in Virginia, over a year could go by without us seeing them—though we kept in regular contact by letter and phone.

One Christmas, they sent us a close-up picture of just the two of them. The photograph perfectly framed their exuberantly smiling faces, and guess what? The resemblance was uncanny. If you ever wondered what a red-headed, fair-skinned, Japanese woman would look like, I have a picture you just have to see!

How does this happen? Researchers from Yale University studied this phenomenon and determined that people who live with each other for a long period of time often begin to unconsciously mimic each other's facial expressions. This becomes a form of "facial body-building," literally shaping the way we look, so that even my friends, Rob and Jill, could start to look alike.

In the same way, as we practice the attitudes and virtues of Christ, we are transformed to look like Him. They shape our spirits and souls until, however faintly, we begin to resemble our Savior and Lord.

It might sound somewhat odd for me to admit this, but writing this book has changed my life. Studying the virtues of Jesus—looking intently into His attitudes and actions—and reading from the works of Christians who have learned to practice them, as well as meditating on the Scriptures that showcase them, has been one of the highlights of my spiritual life thus far. I have been challenged in ways that I've never been challenged before. I've experienced renewal in areas that were long riddled with defeat and lethargy.

Why? Because the virtues show me how I can slowly begin to resemble Christ. I've been particularly moved by two truths. The first is that real change *is* possible. It's not instant. I shouldn't expect a "magic moment" in which God zaps me into holiness once and for all, but there is hope that I can experience Christ through gradual inner change.

The second truth is recognizing that the virtues are something I practice, not something I become. I'll never be completely humble, but I can practice humility. I will never corner the market on generosity, but I can practice being generous. Understanding this has removed me from the strain of perfectionism that so marked my early life in Christ. It has allowed me to have more of a God-centered faith. Jesus calls me to respond to Him *and to leave the results in His hands.*

These two points remind me that I seek to become like Christ under the canopy of grace. The virtues are not a difficult performance we are called to give before a demanding, tyrannical parent, but a life-affirming, soul-refreshing invitation to become persons of integrity—the persons God created us to be.

Because of grace, those areas in my life that have not been marked by virtue can be forgiven as well as changed. Because of grace, I'm not locked into the thornier aspects of my personality. Because of grace, areas once marked by shame can be cleansed, renewed, and remade.

I'm still very much a work in progress, but as long as I'm practicing the virtues, I'm at least headed in the right direction. I've discovered that the glorious pursuit I'm after is to be buried in God's heart. I long to feel His power coursing through me. I ache to sense

His patience, fortitude, gentleness, and surrender giving me a new inner strength.

And then, perhaps, one day someone will meet me—or you—and though they won't immediately think of Jesus, they might, after they've left, be reminded of something, and hours later come to realize that there was a hint, a shadow, an imperfect reflection demonstrating God's life in me and in you.

God wants to give you your life back, your *true* life. Not the one you've tarnished, abused, and neglected, but the one He designed while you were yet in your mother's womb. To fully experience this, we may have to go back over these chapters and virtues time and time again. Certainly we will have to write new chapters and explore new virtues. But if we keep looking into the mirror of the virtues of Christ, transformation will take place.

As we busy ourselves on this journey, we may be caught by surprise, for eventually eternity will overtake us and the glorious pursuit will become a glorious reality. As John puts it, this world will be peeled away and our change will be complete: "But we know that when he appears, we shall be like him, for we shall see him as he is. Everyone who has this hope in him purifies himself, just as he is pure" (1 John 3:2-3).

Will you begin this journey today?

NOTES

Section One: The Soul of Spiritual Formation

Chapter One: Getting Your Life Back
1. C. S. Lewis, *The Screwtape Letters* (New York: The Macmillan Co., 1951), p. 68.
2. John 10:10.
3. Lewis, p. 64.
4. Peter Kreeft, *Back to Virtue* (San Francisco: Ignatius Press, 1992), p. 64.

Chapter Two: The Holy Bridge
1. Martin Luther, cited in *From Glory to Glory* by Robin Boisvert and C. J. Mahaney (Gaithersburg, MD: PDI Publishing, 1993).
2. The danger is this: Prayer apart from Christ is powerless and ineffective. Prayer alone does not connect us with God, unless our hearts have been transformed through the applied work of Christ. In the same way, virtues do not bring us into God's presence unless a prior work of the Holy Spirit has created in us a new heart. *Assuming God has given us new life*, both prayer and practicing the virtues can become powerful bridges of intimacy.

Chapter Three: The Glorious Pursuit
1. John Climacus, *The Ladder of Divine Ascent*, Trans. by Colm Luibheid and Norman Russell (New York: Paulist Press, 1982), p. 209.
2. John Owen, cited in *From Glory to Glory*, p. 44.
3. Lewis, p. 15.
4. Jonathan Edwards, *Religious Affections* (Minneapolis: Bethany, 1996), p. 8.
5. Edwards, p. 164-165.
6. Edwards, p. 8.
7. Edwards, p. 167.

Section Two: The Classical Virtues

Chapter Four: Living Where You Are (Humility, Part One)
1. Climacus, p. 83.
2. John Calvin, *Institutes of the Christian Religion* (Philadelphia: Westminster Press, 1960), II.2.11.
3. Edwards, p. 128. William Law urges us to make humility the constant, chief subject of your devotion. William Law, *A Serious Call to a Devout and Holy Life* (New York: Paulist Press, 1978), p. 278.

4. Andrew Murray, *Humility* (Springdale, PA: Whitaker House, 1982), p. 24.
5. John 15:5.
6. Murray, p. 59.
7. Cited in Edwards, p. 129
8. Psalm 18:27.
9. Psalm 25:9.
10. Psalm 147:6.
11. Psalm 149:4.
12. Titus 3:2.
13. John 13:1-17.
14. Kreeft, p. 100.
15. John 13:3.
16. Lewis, p. 73.
17. 1 Peter 5:6, emphasis added.

Chapter Five: The Beautiful Spirit (Humility, Part Two)
1. James Thomas Flexner, *Washington: The Indispensable Man* (New York: Mentor Books, 1979), p. 177.
2. Flexner, pp. 177-178.
3. 1 Peter 5:5.
4. James 4:10; Isaiah 26:4-5.
5. Edwards, p. 127.
6. Hosea 13:6.
7. John 5:19; I'm indebted to Andrew Murray for collecting these verses.
8. John 7:16.
9. John 8:28.
10. J. C. Ryle, *Thoughts for Young Men* (Amityville, NY: Calvary Press, 1996), p. 24.
11. Jeanne Guyon, *Experiencing the Depths of Jesus Christ* (Auburn, ME: The Seedsowers, 1975), p. 16.
12. Isaiah 64:6.
13. Murray, p. 44.
14. John of the Cross, *John of the Cross: Selected Writings*, Ed. By Kieran Kavanaugh (New York: Paulist Press), p. 192.
15. Murray, p. 46.

Chapter Six: Resting in the Current (Surrender)
1. Mark 9:49, NKJV.
2. Philippians 4:12, NIV.
3. Compare Hebrews 11.
4. Philippians 4:7.
5. John 21:19-22.
6. Matthew 2:10-11.
7. Romans 1:1.
8. Ephesians 3:7; Colossians 1:23; Titus 1:1.
9. Lewis, cited in Kreeft, p. 101.
10. Guyon, pp. 37-38.
11. Romans 8:17, emphasis added.
12. Guyon, p. 38.
13. Guyon, p. 39.
14. Guyon, p. 43.
15. Guyon, p. 45.
16. Climacus, p. 106.
17. Guyon, p. 141, emphasis added.
18. Romans 8:29.

Chapter Seven: Freedom from Within (Detachment)
1. Francis de Sales, *Introduction to a Devout Life* (New York: Frederick Pustet & Co.), p. 19.
2. Psalm 37:4.
3. John of the Cross, p. 72.
4. John Owen, *Sin and Temptation* (Minneapolis: Bethany, 1996), p. 122.
5. Owen, p. 64.
6. John of the Cross, pp. 64-65.
7. John of the Cross, p. 66.
8. John of the Cross, p. 70.
9. François Fénelon, *Christian Perfection* (Minneapolis: Bethany, 1975), p. 13.
10. John of the Cross, p. 71.
11. John of the Cross, p. 79.
12. John of the Cross, p. 79.
13. In my book, *Sacred Pathways*, I list nine different spiritual temperaments, which are really nine different ways to build your love relationship with God. You might look there if you need some more insight in this regard.

Chapter Eight: The Energy of Your Soul (Love)
1. Stephen Ambrose, *D-Day June 6, 1944* (New York: Simon & Schuster, 1994).
2. Matthew 3:10.
3. Guyon, p. 108.
4. Luke 7:36-50.
5. Edwards, p. 9.
6. Matthew 22:37.
7. Edwards, p. 10.
8. Edwards, p. 10.
9. Philippians 1:21.
10. Climacus, p. 286.
11. Hebrews 3:8, NKJV.
12. Psalm 119:32, NKJV, emphasis added.
13. No one that I know of has written so capably about this as has Jonathan Edwards in his book, *Religious Affections*. If this has been a weak area in your life, I highly recommend Edwards' book as a follow-up.
14. Climacus, p. 77.
15. John Owen, *Sin and Temptation* (Minneapolis: Bethany House, 1996), p. 84.
16. Climacus, p. 287.

Chapter Nine: Safe Relationships (Chastity)
1. Eric Schlosser, The Business of Pornography, *"U.S. News and World Report,"* February 10, 1997, p. 43.
2. Schlosser, p. 44.
3. Kreeft, p. 165.
4. Kreeft, p. 166.
5. Climacus, p. 172.
6. Kreeft, p. 180.
7. Lewis H. Lapham, "In the Garden of Tabloid Delight," *Harpers*, August 1997, p. 39.
8. Compare Romans 1:25.
9. Climacus, p. 179.
10. Titus 1:15.
11. Dr. Dan Allender and Dr. Tremper Longman III, *Bold Love* (Colorado Springs, Colo.: NavPress, 1992), p. 101.
12. Allender, p. 103.
13. See Allender, pp. 102-103.

14. Allender, p. 101.
15. Thomas Aquinas, cited in Kreeft, p. 156.
16. Climacus, p. 171.
17. Kreeft, p. 167.
18. Kreeft, p. 167.
19. 1 Corinthians 7:3-5.
20. Hebrews 13:4.
21. 1 Corinthians 7:2.
22. Lewis, pp. 94-95.

Chapter Ten: Positive Possession (Generosity)
1. Ron and Nancy Goor, *Pompeii: Exploring a Roman Ghost Town* (New York: Thomas Crowell, 1986), p. 47.
2. Kreeft, p. 109.
3. Lewis, p. 143.
4. Acts 20:35.
5. 1 Timothy 6:9-10.
6. Luke 6:38.
7. Matthew 10:8.

Chapter Eleven: Awakened Living (Vigilance)
1. Deuteronomy 4:9.
2. 1 Kings 2:4, emphasis added.
3. Psalm 39:1.
4. Matthew 26:41, emphsis added.
5. Luke 12:15.
6. Luke 21:8.
7. Ryle, p. 33.
8. Climacus, p. 196.
9. Climacus, p. 197.
10. Ryle, p. 31.
11. Climacus, pp. 115, 117.
12. Compare Matthew 13:39; Mark 4:15; Luke 22:31; Ephesians 4:27; 2 Timothy 2:26; James 4:7.
13. Owen, p. 122.
14. Owen, p. 122.
15. Ryle, p. 15.
16. Owen, p. 7.
17. Proverbs 3:5-6.
18. Guyon, p. 74.
19. Lewis, p. 25.
20. Ryle, p. 48.
21. Ryle, p. 49.
22. Thomas Kelly, *A Testament of Devotion* (New York: Harper & Row, 1941; HarperSanFrancisco, 1992), pp. 13-14.

Chapter Twelve: Realistic Expectations (Patience)
1. Cited in *U. S. News & World Report*, 11/11/96, p. 16.
2. Drs. Redford and Virginia Williams, *Anger Kills* (New York: Harper Perennial, 1994), p. xiii.
3. James 4:1-2a.
4. Climacus, p. 216.
5. Climacus, p. 234.

6. Romans 12:12.
7. Guyon, p. 141.
8. 1 Timothy 1:16.
9. Hebrews 6:12.
10. Guyon, p. 140.
11. Revelation 1:9.

Chapter Thirteen: Pure Perception (Discernment)
1. These stories were taken from Peter Howard, *Frank Buchman's Secret* (London: Heinemann, 1961).
2. Edwards, p. 105.
3. Edwards, p. 107.
4. Climacus, p. 229.
5. Matthew 7:29.
6. Edwards, p. 109.
7. Matthew 6:22-23.
8. Peter Howard, *Britain and the Beast* (London: Heinemann, 1963), pp. 124-126.
9. Howard, *Frank Buchman's Secret*, p. 94.
10. Howard, *Frank Buchman's Secret*, p. 25.
11. Howard, *Frank Buchman's Secret*, p. 26.
12. Romans 1:21, emphasis added.
13. Edwards, p. 113.
14. Edwards, p. 124.
15. Miles Davis with Quincy Troupe, *Miles: The Autobiography* (New York: Touchstone Books, 1989), p.10.
16. Matthew 5:27-28.
17. Matthew 5:21-22.
18. James 4:7.
19. 1 Peter 1:13.
20. Ecclesiastes 7:25.

Chapter Fourteen: Exuberant Living (Thankfulness)
1. From a personal interview
2. *William Law: A Serious Call to a Devout and Holy Life* (New York: Paulist Press, 1978), p. 218.
3. Romans 1:21, emphasis added.
4. Psalm 100:4.

Chapter Fifteen: Caressing Life (Gentleness)
1. 1 Thessalonians 2:7.
2. Edwards, p. 144.
3. Matthew 25:24-25.
4. Zechariah 9:9; Matthew 21:5.
5. 2 Corinthians 10:1.
6. 2 Timothy 2:25.

Chapter Sixteen: Courageous Living (Fortitude)
1. Robert Kotlowitz, *Before Their Time* (New York: Alfred A. Knopf, 1997), p. 16.
2. Genesis 15:1.
3. Genesis 26:24.
4. Numbers 21:34.
5. Joshua 1:9, NKJV.

6. Matthew 1:20.
7. Acts 18:9.
8. William Shakespeare, *Julius Caesar,* Act 2, Scene 2.
9. Kreeft, pp. 181-182.
10. Edwards, p. 147.
11. Luke 12:4-5.
12. Joni is a quadriplegic, yet she has ministered to millions of people through her inspirational paintings, books, music, and speeches.

Chapter Seventeen: Enlarged Living (Obedience)
1. Matthew 5:6, emphasis added.
2. *Wall Street Journal,* unsigned article, January 29, 1992, p. 1.
3. Compare Matthew 7:21-23; 25:44-46.
4. Jeremiah 17:9.
5. 1 Corinthians 4:4.
6. Edwards, p. 174.
7. Edwards, p. 179.
8. Edwards, pp. 179-180, emphasis added.
9. John 14:15.
10. Edwards, p. 181, emphasis added.
11. 2 Kings 8:7-15.
12. Ryle, p. 64.
13. Melanie Wells, "Endorser-Mentor Matchup Becoming Part of the Game," *USA Today,* January 8, 1998, B-1, B-2.
14. Psalm 1:2.
15. Romans 12:9, NKJV.
16. Ryle, p. 67.
17. John of the Cross, p. 75.

Chapter Eighteen: The Renewal of Faith (Penitence)
1. Matthew 3:2.
2. Matthew 4:17.
3. Ezekiel 9:2-6, NKJV.
4. Matthew 5:3-4.
5. John 10:10.
6. Kreeft, p. 95.
7. Kreeft, p. 95.
8. *Sports Illustrated,* June 11, 1990.
9. Joel 2:12-13, NKJV.
10. Climacus, p. 124.
11. Climacus, p. 146.
12. Climacus, p. 147.
13. Climacus, p. 130.
14. Climacus, p. 140.
15. Climacus, p. 141.
16. Kreeft, p. 101.
17. Luke 23:43.

AUTHOR

GARY THOMAS is a writer and the founder and director of the Center for Evangelical Spirituality, a publishing and speaking ministry that integrates Scripture, church history, and the Christian classics. His books include *The Glorious Pursuit* (NavPress, 1998), *Sacred Pathways* (chosen by World magazine as one of the top ten books of 1996), and *Seeking the Face of God* (Thomas Nelson, 1994). He is also one of the contributors to the Spiritual Formation Bible, to be published by Zondervan in 1999.

Gary graduated cum laude with a Bachelor of Arts in English literature from Western Washington University, and he holds a master's degree with a concentration in systematic theology from Regent College in Vancouver, B.C., where he studied under Dr. J. I. Packer.

He has had over seventy articles published by numerous national magazines, including *Christianity Today, Moody, Marriage Partnership, New Man, Discipleship Journal, Charisma,* and *World,* among others.

Gary has been a featured guest on numerous radio and television programs, and his speaking assignments take him all over the United States, where he addresses the nature of the spiritual life. He is married, has three children, and lives in Bellingham, Washington.

To contact Gary Thomas or to learn more about the Center for Evangelical Spirituality, write P.O. Box 29417, Bellingham, WA 98228-1417; fax (360) 647-1364; or www.garythomas.com.

GENERAL EDITOR

DALLAS WILLARD is a professor in the school of philosophy at the University of Southern California in Los Angeles. He has been at USC since 1965, where he was director of the school of philosophy from 1982 to 1985. He has also taught at the University of Wisconsin (Madison), where he received his Ph.D. in 1964, and has held visiting appointments at UCLA (1969) and the University of Colorado (1984).

His philosophical publications are mainly in the areas of epistemology, the philosophy of mind and of logic, and on the philosophy of Edmund Husserl, including extensive translations of Husserl's early writings from German into English. His *Logic and the Objectivity of Knowledge,* a study on Husserl's early philosophy, appeared in 1984.

Dr. Willard also lectures and publishes in religion. *In Search of Guidance* was published in 1984 (second edition in 1993), and *The Spirit of the Disciplines* was released in 1988.

He is married to Jane Lakes Willard, a marriage and family counselor with offices in Van Nuys and Canoga Park, California. They have two children, John and Rebecca, and live in Chatsworth, California.

EDITOR

DAVID HAZARD is the editor of spiritual formation books for NavPress. He is also the editor of the classic devotional series, *Rekindling the Inner Fire*, and writes the monthly column, "Classic Christianity" for *Charisma* magazine.

For more than seventeen years, David has held various positions with Christian publishing houses, from editorial director to associate publisher. As a writer, he has contributed numerous internationally best-selling books to contemporary Christian publishing, some of which have been published in more than twenty languages worldwide. As an editor, David has developed more than two hundred books.

For the past twelve years, his special focus and study has been in the classic writings of Christianity, the formation of early Christian doctrine, and Christian spirituality.

IF YOU LIKED THE GLORIOUS PURSUIT, BE SURE TO CHECK OUT THESE OTHER BOOKS IN THE NAVPRESS SPIRITUAL FORMATION LINE.

In His Image

Is it possible to be like Jesus in today's world? This book examines what it means to be like Christ, challenging readers to follow Him wholeheartedly and be transformed in the process.
By Michael Wilkins
ISBN-13: 978-1-57683-000-0
ISBN-10: 1-57683-000-4

Love Your God with All Your Mind

Have you really thought about your faith? This book examines the role of reason in faith, helping believers use their intellect to further God's kingdom.
By J. P. Moreland
ISBN-13: 978-1-57683-016-1
ISBN-10: 1-57683-016-0

Follow Me

Follow Me examines the kingdom of heaven, challenging readers to examine the kingdoms they set up—things like money, relationships, or power—that keep them from truly following Jesus.
By Jan David Hettinga
ISBN-13: 978-0-89109-982-6
ISBN-10: 0-89109-982-4

To order copies, visit your local Christian bookstore, call NavPress at 1-800-366-7788, or log on to www.navpress.com.
To locate a Christian bookstore near you, call 1-800-991-7747.

NAVPRESS
BRINGING TRUTH TO LIFE
www.navpress.com